Inclusive Hymns for Liberation, Peace, and Justice

Jann Aldredge-Clanton
with composer Larry E. Schultz

All rights reserved. With the purchase of 10 or more copies of this book, unlimited permission to reproduce the hymns is given. With purchase of fewer than 10, for permission to reproduce the hymns please contact OneLicense.net, CCLI.com, or LicenSingOnline.org. Copyright information must be included at the bottom of any reproduced hymn along with this phrase: From *Inclusive Hymns for Liberation, Peace, and Justice* (Eakin Press, 2011).

Copyright © 2011
By Jann Aldredge-Clanton & Larry E. Schultz
Published By Eakin Press
An Imprint of Wild Horse Media Group
P.O. Box 331779
Fort Worth, Texas 76163
1-817-344-7036
www.EakinPress.com
ALL RIGHTS RESERVED
1 2 3 4 5 6 7 8 9
Paperback ISBN 978-1-68179-287-3
Hardback ISBN 978-1-68179-288-0
eBook ISBN 978-1-68179-289-7

CONTENTS

INTRODUCTION.. 7

LIBERATION

1. O Loving Creator, We Labor with You
2. Sister-Brother, Peaceful Spirit
3. Praise Wisdom in Our Hearts
4. Ruah, the Spirit-Source of All
5. Behold Shekhinah Leading
6. Arise and Celebrate

JUSTICE AND PEACEMAKING

7. Awake to Work for Peace on Earth
8. When Will Justice Flow Like Waters?
9. Shekhinah Is Our Dwelling Place
10. Celebrate the Works of Wisdom
11. Wisdom, Sophia, Joins in Our Labor
12. Come, Ruah, Spirit, Bring New Life

CARE OF CREATION

13. The Music Is Ringing
14. Creation Calls to Us for Help

15. Our Mother-Father, Friend and Source
16. All the World with Beauty Shines

ONENESS

17. We Long to Dwell in Unity
18. Sacred Darkness Dwelling
19. We Praise You, Holy Other

PARTNERSHIP AND COMMUNITY

20. Celebrate Our Life Together
21. We Gather Here to Pray
22. We Come to Tell Our Stories

CALL AND MISSION

23. Wisdom Calls Us to Her Mission
24. Ruah, the Spirit, Gives Each One a Song
25. Come Now, and Follow Wisdom
26. Midwife Divine Is Bringing Life to Birth
27. Wisdom Graciously Gives to All
28. Mother Eagle in the Sky

LAMENT

29. Where Are You When We Need You?
30. How Long Will People Suffer?

COMFORT AND HEALING

31. El Shaddai Will Come to Help Us
32. Our Shepherd Gives Us All We Need
33. Come, Sophia, to Calm Our Souls
34. Our Souls Find Rest and Comfort
35. Our Shepherd Comes in Loving Care
36. Come, Christ-Sophia, Come

DEDICATION OF CHILDREN

37. O Loving Maker, Bless This Child, We Pray
38. Great Creator, Bless This Child

THANKSGIVING AND CELEBRATION

39. O Holy One, We Sing Your Praise
40. We Praise the Works of Wisdom
41. Celebrate the Good Creation
42. Composer of All the Music We Hear
43. Ruah, Creator, Gave Birth to Us All

ADVENT

44. Holy Wisdom Comes to Earth
45. Come to Our World, O Christ-Sophia
46. Come to Free Us, Christ-Sophia

CHRISTMAS

47. Come, Celebrate and Sing
48. Celebrate Sophia's Birth
49. Sing of Peace, Holy Peace

EPIPHANY

50. Star of Wonder, Star of Wisdom
51. Ancient Wisdom, Mother of Earth
52. O Holy Darkness, Source of Life

EASTER

53. We Are an Easter People
54. Come, Easter People, Come, Rejoice

PENTECOST

55. Ruah, Spirit, Come Today
56. Waiting Now with Expectation

Notes	85
Topical Index of Hymns	93
Index of Scripture References	117
Index of Composers, Authors, and Sources	119
Alphabetical Index of Tunes	121
Metrical Index of Tunes	123
Index of Titles	125

INTRODUCTION

"The words we sing in worship matter." So begins the introduction to *Inclusive Hymns for Liberating Christians*.[1] Now five years later as I write the introduction to this new collection of hymns, my belief in the power of worship language is even stronger. We can make a difference for peace, justice, and liberation in our world through the words we sing in worship. Words matter. Words we use in worship carry great power because of the sacred value given to them. Words we sing in worship have the greatest power to shape our beliefs and actions because the music embeds the words in our memories.

The intense feelings evoked by including female divine names in worship reveal just how powerful words can be. I have seen tears stream down the faces of women as they sing hymns with female divine names and then say that this is the first time they have truly felt they are created in the divine image. Others have commented that hymns with *Ruah*,[2] *Sophia*,[3] *Shekhinah*,[4] "Mother Eagle" and other female divine names nourish and empower them as nothing else in worship ever has. After singing *Imagine God! A Children's Musical Exploring and Expressing Images of God*,[5] a little girl said that her favorite divine image in the musical is Lady Wisdom because She makes her feel strong. A little boy said that Wisdom and Mother Eagle are his favorite divine images because they are "very creative." Men, as well as women, have expressed appreciation for the power of the Divine Feminine to heal sexism, racism, heterosexism, and classism. Men have advocated for inclusive language in worship not only for social justice, but also to bring wholeness to their lives and to deepen their spiritual experience. People who have felt alienated from the Christian tradition because of exclusively masculine divine images have found a new connection through the discovery of the Divine Feminine in the tradition.

Thus *Ruah*, the Creative Spirit, has continued to call me to write hymn lyrics with inclusive, expansive language. Sometimes the words come in a flash of inspiration. Other hymns take more struggle to find the best images, rhymes, and meter to convey the meaning. Writing a hymn for me is an act of faith. It takes faith to begin a hymn and faith to keep working with it even when I feel blocked. It takes faith to claim the Divine within me, working with me through the often slow process of writing. In this new collection, the hymn "O Loving Creator, We Labor with You" expresses this process of co-creation.

Inspiration and support have also come through faith communities, and I am indeed grateful to them. Not long after the publication of *Inclusive Hymns for Liberating Christians*, Stacy Boorn, pastor of Ebenezer Lutheran Church in San Francisco, invited me to be the keynote speaker for the first Faith and Feminism/Womanist/Mujerista Conference, which the church sponsored in 2007. This conference and subsequent conferences have featured songs from *Inclusive Hymns for Liberating Christians*, and all participants have received this hymnal. Ebenezer Lutheran Church also draws from this hymnal for worship services, and commissioned me to write some of the hymns included in this new collection. Pullen Memorial Baptist Church in Raleigh, North Carolina, has included many of my hymns in worship and has supported Minister of Music Larry Schultz's collaboration with me on this new collection, *Inclusive Hymns for Liberation, Peace, and Justice*, and on the earlier hymnal. In addition, the Pullen choirs worked with Larry in recording a CD of many of the hymns in the first hymnal. New Wineskins Community[6] in Dallas, Texas, "congregation-tested" most of the hymns in this new collection as well as those in the earlier hymnal. This community continues to encourage me to create hymns and then sings them with enthusiasm in our worship services. Other Dallas communities have supported my hymn writing: Church in the Cliff, formerly CityChurch; Grace United Methodist Church; Royal Lane Baptist Church; Northridge Presbyterian Church; East Dallas Christian Church; Highland Park United Methodist Church; Perkins School of Theology; and Pastoral Counseling and Education Center. Also, I often hear from people around the country who express appreciation for the first hymnal and ask me to keep writing hymns.

This new hymn collection comes then as a response to the Spirit's calling through many individuals and communities. And the pressing needs in our world continue to compel me to write inclusive hymns with themes of liberation, peace, and justice.

Since many traditional and current hymns contain exclusive language and theology that inadvertently support injustice, congregations are seeking hymns that more nearly reflect their beliefs. The lyrics of the hymns in this collection draw from the prophetic, liberating tradition in Scripture. Biblical themes, phrases, and images form the foundation for these hymns, and I have included biblical references with the hymns.

Social Justice

Today, more than ever, we need to hear the words of the prophet Amos: "Let justice roll down like waters, and righteousness like an everflowing stream" (Amos 5:24). Social justice is a major theme of this collection of hymns. One hymn begins with the question: "When will justice flow like waters, bringing healing to the earth?"

Oppression of women and girls around the world continues at alarming rates. In the U.S. alone, every fifteen seconds a woman is battered.[7] One in three women in the world experiences some kind of abuse in her lifetime.[8] Worldwide, an estimated four million women and girls each year are bought and sold into prostitution, slavery, or marriage.[9] "More girls have been killed in the last fifty years, precisely because they were girls, than men were killed in all the battles of the twentieth century. More girls are killed in this routine 'gendercide' in any one decade than people were slaughtered in all the genocides of the twentieth century."[10] Seventy percent of the world's poor are women.[11] There are many more alarming statistics on worldwide violence and discrimination against women and girls.

We can work in many ways to end this violence and injustice. One vital way is to help change the patriarchal structures that give rise to this oppression. Words shape our value system and our whole culture. We can give powerful support to the sacred value of women and girls by adding biblical feminine words to our language for Deity, like "Mother," *Ruah, Sophia, Shekhinah* and *El Shaddai*.[12] When we include female names for Deity, then women and girls are seen in Her image and thus respected and valued, instead of battered and abused. Female divine names and images lay the theological foundation for a more just world.

Worship and social justice cannot be separated. The prophet Amos denounces those who offer sacrifices and songs in worship while oppressing people. How can we act fairly toward people when we exclude or devalue them in our most sacred rituals and language? How can we profess to love everyone when we leave out more than half of humanity in our naming of divinity? How can we say that everyone is created in the divine image when we leave out female divine images in our worship? Sponsoring a shelter for battered women while our worship sanctions a male-dominated society is like putting a Band-Aid on a gaping wound that we inflicted. We have to keep putting on the Band-Aids, but this cannot suffice. Balancing female and male divine images will contribute to the breaking down of patriarchal structures that cause the violence and injustice.

We can sing justice into reality. The hymns in this collection are inclusive for humanity and for divinity. They include sisters as well as brothers, and use gender balanced divine names, such as "Mother-Father," "Sister-Brother," and "Christ-Sophia"[13] to symbolize partnership and equality in all relationships. These hymns also give "affirmative action" to biblical female names for Deity, such as *Sophia* and

Ruah, because they have been ignored for centuries and because they continue to be excluded from most worship services and hymnals. These hymns are intended to help overcome this injustice and bring balance to worship.

The hymns in this collection also contribute to racial justice by changing the traditional symbolism of darkness as evil or ominous. These hymns affirm the sacred value of people of color by giving positive meanings to images of darkness. For example, "O Holy Darkness, Source of Life" celebrates darkness as the sacred power that creates and restores. The first stanza proclaims the blessings and beauty of darkness:

> O Holy Darkness, Source of Life,
> Your blessings flow throughout the earth;
> Your beauty stirs us all to strive
> with You creation to revive,
> and bring Your seeds to birth.

The hymn "We Praise the Works of Wisdom" brings darkness and light together in the creative process: "The works of Wisdom flourish through darkness and through light."

This hymn collection also seeks to contribute to justice for LGBTQ persons, who continue to be excluded and oppressed in church and society. Often they are labeled as "other." One hymn images the Divine as "Other," beginning with this stanza:

> We praise You, Holy Other, divinity in all;
> our love for one another fulfills Your highest call.
> When we are labeled "other" by custom's narrow norms,
> show us our sacred value, Your image in each form.

We can sing justice into reality for all those who are made to feel "other" because of sexual orientation, gender, race, class, and/or disability. "When Will Justice Flow Like Waters?" laments these various forms of injustice and calls us to work for change: "Still injustice based on gender, race, and class and stifling norms stirs us all to loving action, joining You to bring reform." The hymn ends with this prayer:

> Holy Wisdom, send us forward, spreading Good News everywhere;
> freedom's doors will swing wide open, as with You we dream and dare.
> Joining You to end oppression, we break walls to bring release;
> all creation blossoms fully on Your wondrous paths of peace.

Peace

From justice flows peace. Sexism, racism, classism, heterosexism, discrimination against people with disabilities, religious discrimination, and all forms of injustice impede peace. The hymns in this collection link justice and peace, calling for an end to war among nations and in city streets and for the end of violence in homes and institutions. For example, in the hymn "Awake to Work for Peace on Earth" Wisdom calls us to join Her work of peace and justice:

Still Wisdom calls to everyone to join Her work of peace;
now let us rise to follow Her so justice may increase.
We all are broken from the wounds that violence brings to earth;
we all are longing for the day our wholeness is rebirthed.

The biblical image of Divine Wisdom is prominent here and in many other hymns in this collection. To counteract the prevalent images of violence and death in our culture, Wisdom is an image of peace and life. "Her ways are ways of pleasantness, and all her paths are peace. She is a tree of life to those who lay hold of her; those who hold her fast are called happy" (Proverbs 3:17-18).

Internal peace, as well as external peace, is a focus of *Inclusive Hymns for Liberation, Peace, and Justice*. Peace within individuals will contribute to peace in our world. Through pain and suffering and challenges, we long for inner peace to sustain us. The hymn "Come, Sophia, to Calm Our Souls" is a prayer to Divine Wisdom for comfort and peace to sustain and restore us. "El Shaddai Will Come to Help Us" affirms hope and peace in the midst of pain and sorrow, ending with this stanza:

El Shaddai with deep compassion will forever with us stay;
giving guidance through each challenge, She will show the healing way.
Helping all our fears release, She will lead to hope and peace.

Liberation

Liberation also goes hand in hand with social justice. Many of the hymns in this collection sing of freedom from discrimination and injustice in any form. The hope is to "loose the bonds of injustice, to undo the thongs of the yoke, to let the oppressed go free, and to break every yoke" (Isaiah 58:6). In the hymn "Behold Shekhinah Leading" we sing of taking part in bringing this freedom:

Behold Shekhinah leading in liberating all;
She guides us as we join Her in breaking down each wall.
Her glory shines around us, within us, and above
to show the way to healing through Her transforming love.

These hymns sing of freedom from stifling customs and forms. Many of our songs in worship, because of their exclusivity, have kept us in bondage to injustices in our culture. The hymns in this collection support freedom from sexism, racism, heterosexism, and other injustices. The act of singing new inclusive words will help to free us from slavery to tradition and to free us all to claim our gifts.

This hymn collection also encourages internal freedom to find our own voices, follow our call, and become all we're created to be in the divine image. The hymn "We Come to Tell Our Stories" affirms the power of each person's story and gifts to bring liberation within faith communities: "O Sister-Brother Spirit, we hear Your gentle call to share our sacred stories, that liberate us all."

One hymn begins with a prayer for freedom, bringing justice and peace and liberation together:

Come to free us, Christ-Sophia, through Your just and peaceful way;
for Your Advent we have waited, hoping for a better day.
Violence ending, conflict mending, nature tending, freedom sending:
Christ-Sophia, come today.

Care of Creation

Not only human beings but the whole creation longs for freedom. All created beings need our work of justice and peace. Care of creation is another prominent theme of *Inclusive Hymns for Liberation, Peace, and Justice*.

Just as diversity contributes to healthy human communities, diversity helps all of creation. Ecologists stress the importance of maintaining biodiversity, the variety of life forms, to sustain the earth. A diversity of species of plants, animals, and micro-organisms contributes to a healthy earth. Each species, no matter how small, has an important role to play. Greater species diversity ensures natural sustainability for all life forms. The massive BP oil spill in the Gulf of Mexico[14] is just one of the human activities that has damaged ecosystems and threatened a variety of species.

This collection of hymns celebrates the variety of life forms and calls for conservation. In the hymn "Our Mother-Father, Friend and Source," we sing our gratitude for the diversity of creation: "roaring lions," "flying squirrels," "golden trees," "leaping frogs," "gliding swans," "all creatures large and small." The hymn ends with a prayer for power to help in conserving life:

> Creative Spirit, give us power to work with You for life,
> conserving all Your precious gifts, so earth will long survive.
> Renewing, caring, joining You to bring creation new,
> we sing with clapping sea and sky to praise Your wondrous view.

For the enormous tasks of renewing and saving our environment, we can find power through partnership. A major focus of this hymn collection is partnership—partnership in the care of creation, as well as partnership in other peace and justice work. We find strength as we join with one another, with the Divine, and with all creation. One of the hymns begins with this call to join together in saving the earth:

> Creation calls to us for help; the earth cries out for care.
> The Loving Spirit shows the way to save earth's treasures rare.
> Then let us work together now, our gifts to freely share.

Oneness

Coming together, working together, unity—all are celebrated in this hymn collection. Oneness is another major theme of *Inclusive Hymns for Liberation, Peace, and Justice*. These hymns encourage diverse people to come together as one, and many of the hymns are appropriate for interfaith settings. The hymn "We Praise You, Holy Other" celebrates "our oneness that breaks down every wall."

One of the hymns in this collection draws from Psalm 133:1: "How very good and pleasant it is when kindred live together in unity!" The hymn begins with a longing and a prayer for unity:

> We long to dwell in unity,
> our varied gifts in harmony;
> come, Sister-Brother Spirit, come,
> and show the way to make us one.

In today's context of globalization, the recognition of our oneness can help overcome violence and end wars that continue to be fought over religious and cultural differences. Our very lives may depend on our acceptance of the interconnectedness of all nations and all people. The last stanza of the hymn "Ruah, the Spirit-Source of All" proclaims the life-giving power of oneness:

> Spirit of Oneness, path to life,
> opens our hearts, our hope revives,
> that we may see a wider view,
> all of creation shining new.

Hymns in this collection sing of our oneness with all creation. The realization of our connection with all life on earth empowers our environmental activism. The hymn "Sister-Brother, Peaceful Spirit" calls us to "nurture all creation" as we "tune our music to the oneness of us all."

Collaboration in Hymn Writing

One of the joys of writing *Inclusive Hymns for Liberation, Peace, and Justice* has come through my continued collaboration with composer Larry E. Schultz. For some of the hymns in this collection Larry wrote fresh arrangements of traditional tunes. For other hymns he has composed original, vibrant music that complements the lyrics. Larry is also an accomplished, published text writer. In this collection you will find several of Larry's creative texts. Larry and I have previously collaborated on *Inclusive Hymns for Liberating Christians; Imagine God! A Children's Musical Exploring and Expressing Images of God; Sing and Dance and Play with Joy! Inclusive Songs for Young Children*; and some anthems.[15]

All hymnody involves collaboration. Lyricists and composers collaborate in writing the hymns. Congregations complete the collaboration by joining in the singing of the hymns. We invite you to join the creative adventure of singing these new hymns and possibly writing new inclusive hymns for worship.

Our hope and prayer is that the hymns in this collection will inspire communities and individuals to take part in the creation of new life. In partnership with the Creative Spirit, we have created these hymns. We pray that they will help create liberation, peace, and justice in our world.

Notes

1. Jann Aldredge-Clanton with Larry E. Schultz, *Inclusive Hymns for Liberating Christians* (Austin: Eakin Press, 2006).
2. *Ruah* is the Hebrew word for "Spirit" in the book of Genesis and elsewhere in the Hebrew Scriptures.
3. *Sophia* is the Greek word for "Wisdom," linked to Christ in the Christian Scriptures.
4. *Shekhinah* is the feminine Hebrew word translated "dwelling" or "settling," and is used to denote the dwelling presence of God and/or the glory of God.

5. Jann Aldredge-Clanton and Larry E. Schultz, *Imagine God! A Children's Musical Exploring and Expressing Images of God* (Dallas, Texas: Choristers Guild, 2004).

6. New Wineskins Community, in Dallas, Texas, explores news ways of seeing divinity and interpreting Scripture so that the spiritual gifts of everyone are equally valued and nurtured. The name "New Wineskins," coming from the metaphor in Matthew 9:17, describes the search for new language and symbols to proclaim the gospel of liberation and shalom. This ecumenical community's rituals include female and male divine names and images to symbolize shared power and responsibility.

7. "Broken Bodies, Shattered Minds: The Global Epidemic of Violence against Women," *International Journal of Epidemiology* 30 (2001): 649-52.

8. United Nations General Assembly, "In-Depth Study on All Forms of Violence against Women: Report of the Secretary General, 2006," A/61/122/Add.1. 6 (July 2006).

9. The United Nations Population Fund, The State of World Population 2000 report, "Lives Together, Worlds Apart: Men and Women in a Time of Change" (2000).

10. Nicholas D. Kristof and Sheryl WuDunn, *Half the Sky: Turning Oppression into Opportunity for Women Worldwide* (New York: Alfred A. Knopf, 2009), p. xvii.

11. Louise Arbour, United Nations High Commissioner for Human Rights, "International Women's Day: Laws and 'Low Intensity' Discrimination Against Women" (March 8, 2008).

12. *El Shaddai* is a Hebrew name translated "God of the Breasts," "the Breasted God," or "God Almighty."

13. "Christ-Sophia" balances the masculine name "Christ" with the feminine name *Sophia* (word for "Wisdom" in the original Greek language of the Christian Scriptures). The name "Christ-Sophia" makes equal connections between male and female, and Jewish and Christian traditions, thus providing a model for partnership rather than dominant-submissive relationships. Writers of the Christian Scriptures link Christ to Wisdom, a female symbol of deity in the Hebrew Scriptures. Wisdom (*Hokmah* in Hebrew) symbolizes creative, redemptive, and healing power. In their efforts to describe this same power in Christ, the apostle Paul and other writers of the Christian Scriptures draw from the picture of female Wisdom in Hebrew Scriptures. Paul refers to Christ as "the power of God and the Wisdom (*Sophia*) of God" (1 Corinthians 1:24), and states that Christ "became for us Wisdom (*Sophia*) from God" (1 Corinthians 1:30). The book of Proverbs describes *Hokmah* as the way, the life, and the path (4:11,22,26). The writer of the Gospel of John refers to Christ as "the way, and the truth, and the life" (John 14:6). What Judaism said of personified female Wisdom, Christian writers came to say of Christ: the image of the invisible God (Colossians 1:15); the radiant light of God's glory (Hebrews 1:3); the one through whom the world was created (John 1:3). See *In Search of the Christ-Sophia: An Inclusive Christology for Liberating Christians* (Twenty-Third Publications, 1995; Eakin Press, 2004) for an elaboration of the connection between Christ and *Sophia* (Wisdom) in Scripture and Christian tradition.

14. The BP oil spill (also referred to as the Gulf of Mexico oil spill, the BP oil disaster, or the Macondo blowout) in the Gulf of Mexico is the largest marine oil spill in the history of the petroleum industry. The spill stemmed from a sea-floor oil gusher that resulted from the April 20, 2010 Deepwater Horizon drilling rig explosion. On July 15, the leak was

stopped by capping the gushing wellhead after it had released about 4.9 million barrels of crude oil.

15. *Inclusive Hymns for Liberating Christians* (Eakin Press, 2006); *Imagine God! A Children's Musical Exploring and Expressing Images of God* (Choristers Guild, 2004); *Sing and Dance and Play with Joy! Inclusive Songs for Young Children* (Lulu, 2009); "Loving Friend of Everyone" (Choristers Guild, 2005); "We Thank you God for Animal Friends" (Choristers Guild, 2007); "Are You Good and Are You Strong?" (Alfred Publishing Co., 2008).

New Creation, Social Justice

1   O Loving Creator, We Labor with You

Isaiah 42:14, 66:13; 2 Corinthians 5:17

1. O Loving Creator, we labor with You to bring forth a world filled with beauty anew. Fresh hope and new strength for our
2. O Loving Creator, within and above, You come as a Mother with comforting love. We join in Your work with the
3. O Loving Creator, we join in Your plan to bring peace and justice throughout every land. We're coming as families, all
4. O Loving Creator, You nurture us all to grow in Your image and answer Your call. As brothers and sisters to-

Words: Jann Aldredge-Clanton
Music: Larry E. Schultz
Words © 2007 Jann Aldredge-Clanton. Music © 2008 Larry E. Schultz.

VESTA
11.11.11.11

New Creation, Social Justice

1a O Loving Creator, We Labor With You

Isaiah 42:14, 66:13; 2 Corinthians 5:17

1. O Loving Creator, we labor with You
to bring forth a world filled with beauty anew.
Fresh hope and new strength for our labor, we pray;
O give us Your vision of glorious days.

2. O Loving Creator, within and above,
You come as a Mother with comforting love.
We join in Your work with the poor and distressed;
as partners we labor that all may be blessed.

3. O Loving Creator, we join in Your plan
to bring peace and justice throughout every land.
We come now as families, all races and kinds,
to offer our gifts, as new freedom we find.

4. O Loving Creator, You nurture us all
to grow in Your image and answer Your call.
As sisters and brothers together on earth,
we labor with You, new creation to birth.

Words: Jann Aldredge-Clanton
Music: Welsh hymn tune
Words © 2007 Jann Aldredge-Clanton.

ST. DENIO
11.11.11.11

Freedom

3 Praise Wisdom in Our Hearts

Proverbs 1:20-23, 3:13-18

1. Praise Wisdom in our hearts; come, rejoicing, praise Her!
   True freedom She imparts; come, rejoicing, praise Her!
   She has been long ignored; now is Her truth explored;
   all earth will be restored; come, rejoicing, praise Her!

2. Praise Wisdom through the years; come, rejoicing, praise Her!
   Now all Her words we hear; come, rejoicing, praise Her!
   She is our guiding Way, leading to better days;
   with us She always stays; come, rejoicing, praise Her!

3. Wisdom has set us free; come, rejoicing, praise Her!
   Now all Her works we see; come, rejoicing, praise Her!
   She is our path to peace; with Her we find release;
   Her love will never cease; come, rejoicing, praise Her!

Words: Jann Aldredge-Clanton
Music: Traditional Spanish melody; arr. Larry E. Schultz
Words © 2009 Jann Aldredge-Clanton. Music arr.© 2010 Larry E. Schultz.

MADRID
6.6.6.6 D

Freedom, Vision

Ruah,* the Spirit-Source of All   4

Genesis 1:1-27; Psalm 85:10, 104:30

1. Ru-ah, the Spirit-Source of all, brings forth creation with Her call. In Her own image made to be, all are creative, wise, and free; all are creative, wise, and free.
2. Ru-ah, the Spirit, in us all, gives us the power to break down walls; so we together work for peace, freedom and justice to increase, freedom and justice to increase.
3. Spirit of Oneness, path to life, opens our hearts, our hope revives, that we may see a wider view, all of creation shining new, all of creation shining new.

Words: Jann Aldredge-Clanton
Music: Frederick M. A. Venua
Words © 2009 Jann Aldredge-Clanton.

PARK STREET
8.8.8.8.8

*Ruah is the word for "Spirit" in the Hebrew Scriptures.

Freedom, Vision

5   Behold Shekhinah* Leading

Exodus 40:34-38, 29:45

1. Be-hold Shekhinah leading in liberating all;
She guides us as we join Her in breaking down each wall.
Her glory shines around us, within us, and above
to show the way to healing through Her transforming love.

2. Shekhinah guides our journey throughout each night and day;
Her paths of truth we follow to just and peaceful ways.
No more will bondage keep us from claiming gifts divine;
for we embrace our power, our sacred treasures mine.

3. The glory of Shekhinah inspires our minds and hearts;
She dwells in all creation with wonders to impart.
Shekhinah gives us visions of new reality,
a world of peace and justice, where all are whole and free.

Words: Jann Aldredge-Clanton
Music: *Gesangbuch*, Wittenberg, 1784
Words © 2009 Jann Aldredge-Clanton

ELLACOMBE
7.6.7.6 D

*Shekhinah is a feminine Hebrew word translated "dwelling" or "settling," and is used to denote the dwelling presence of God and/or the glory of God.

Freedom

Arise and Celebrate

John 8:32; Luke 4:18-19; Galatians 3:28

6

1. A-rise and cel-e-brate; the Truth has set us free, for Christ-So-phi-a helps us be all we are meant to be.
2. As part-ners let us join in set-ting peo-ple free; with Christ-So-phi-a we can bring forth true e-qual-i-ty.
3. To-geth-er we will work that jus-tice all may know; in Christ-So-phi-a all are one, a peace-ful way we show.
4. We rise to cel-e-brate our lib-er-at-ing call; with Christ-So-phi-a we can bring the Good News un-to all.

Words: Jann Aldredge-Clanton
Music: William Henry Walter
Words © 2011 Jann Aldredge-Clanton.

FESTAL SONG
6.6.8.6

Call, Social Justice

7   Awake to Work for Peace on Earth

Proverbs 1:20-24, 3:13-18, 8:20

1. Awake to work for peace on earth through Holy Wisdom's power; come, join together, give our all in this most urgent hour.
2. Still Wisdom calls to everyone to join Her work of peace; now let us rise to follow Her so justice may increase.
3. Rejoice, for Holy Wisdom comes with guidance for each day; She lives within us and above to show the peaceful way.

Words: Jann Aldredge-Clanton
Music: English folk melody; arr. Ralph Vaughan Williams
Words © 2009 Jann Aldredge-Clanton.

KINGSFOLD
8.6.8.6 D (CMD)

Peace, Social Justice

Celebrate the Works of Wisdom   10
Proverbs 1, 3, 8

1. Celebrate the works of Wisdom, shining forth in all that's fair;
   Wisdom shows us peaceful pathways, calling us to dream and dare.
   Like a vision bright and golden, Wisdom comes to light our way,
   bringing us Her gifts most precious, leading to a better day.

2. Wisdom works in every nation, guiding us to live in peace;
   teaching healing care and kindness, She will help all violence cease.
   Wisdom works through men and women, prophets bold throughout the years,
   speaking up for truth and justice, crying out for all to hear.

3. Works of Wisdom bring abundance, lovely works beyond compare;
   Wisdom opens doors of freedom, calling everyone to share.
   Like a tree of life She blossoms, spreading beauty through the earth.
   We can join the work of Wisdom, new creation now to birth.

Words: Jann Aldredge-Clanton
Music: Ludwig van Beethoven

HYMN TO JOY
8.7.8.7 D

Words © 2009 Jann Aldredge-Clanton.

Creativity, Peace
11 Wisdom, Sophia, Joins in Our Labor
Isaiah 42:14; Proverbs 3:13-18

1. Wisdom, Sophia, joins in our labor; She with us freely co-creates life; on this adventure, loving our neighbors, kindness we nurture, ending the strife.
2. Wisdom, Sophia, shares in our sorrows, joining us freely, feeling our pain, caring, caressing, now and tomorrow, giving us blessing, hope to regain.
3. Wisdom, Sophia, gives us new power, helping to free us, bringing us peace; She with us healing that we may flower, beauty revealing, talents released.
4. She is transforming, Wisdom, Sophia, daily reforming, giving new birth; changing and growing, She with us freeing, touching and flowing, nourishing earth.

Words: Jann Aldredge-Clanton
Music: Traditional Gaelic melody

BUNESSAN
5.5.5.4 D

Peace

Come, Ruah,* Spirit, Bring New Life   12

Genesis 1:1-2; Galatians 5:22-23

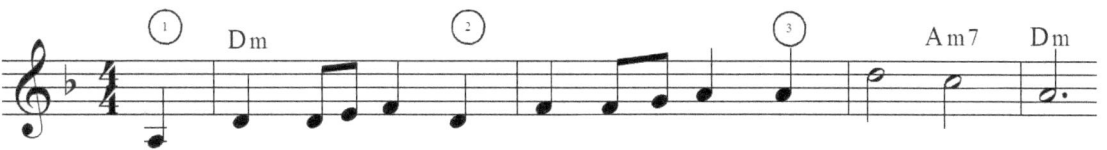

1. Come, Ru - ah, Spir - it, bring new life, bring life to - day;
2. Come, Ru - ah, Spir - it, send Your peace, sha - lom, to - day;

bring life a - new, a wid - er view to all, we pray.
send peace, sha - lom, to all sha - lom, Your peace, we pray.

Words: Jann Aldredge-Clanton
Music: Hebrew melody
Words © 2010 Jann Aldredge-Clanton.

SHALOM
Irregular

Ruah is the word for "Spirit" in the Hebrew Scriptures.
This hymn may be sung in a three-part round.

Care of Creation

14 Creation Calls to Us for Help
Psalm 104:5-32

1. Creation calls to us for help; the earth cries out for care. The Loving Spirit shows the way to save earth's treasures rare. Then let us work together now, our gifts to freely share.

2. Creating Spirit fills the earth with wonders great and small. The streams gush forth in valleys deep, and trees grow green and tall. The roaring lions and sporting whales, the Spirit made them all.

3. Renewing Spirit calls to us to work for saving life. Restoring, caring, joining hands, we help our earth survive. Then let us labor every day, so earth will be revived.

Words: Jann Aldredge-Clanton
Music: attr. Elkanah Kelsay Dare; Wyeth's *Repository of Sacred Music, Part Second*
Words © 2010 Jann Aldredge-Clanton.

MORNING SONG
8.6.8.6.8.6

Oneness

We Long to Dwell in Unity

17

Psalm 133:1; Isaiah 55:12

1. We long to dwell in unity, our varied gifts in harmony; come, Sister-Brother Spirit, come, and show the way to make us one.
2. The Spirit lives within us all, and helps us claim our sacred call; we join to heal divisive ways, creating fair and peaceful days.
3. We shall go out in hope and peace; our finest gifts will be released. Together joyful songs we raise, our Brother-Sister Spirit praise.

Words: Jann Aldredge-Clanton
Music: Traditional Engish melody; arr. Larry E. Schultz
Words © 2010 Jann Aldredge-Clanton; Music arr. © 2011 Larry E. Schultz.

O WALY WALY
8.8.8.8 (LM)

Community, Partnership

20 Celebrate Our Life Together

Micah 6:8; Matthew 23:37; Luke 4:18-19; 1 Corinthians 12:4-11

1. Cel-e-brate our life to-geth-er, giv-ing birth in man-y ways;
Fa-ther-Moth-er Love is with us, lead-ing to a bet-ter day.
E-qual part-ners 'round the ta-ble, fam-ily groups of ev-ery kind
show us how to nur-ture kind-ness, new cre-a-tion's joy to find.

2. Moth-er Christ is call-ing for-ward, long-ing for a peace-ful day,
teach-ing us to free the cap-tives, show-ing us the heal-ing way.
We will o-pen doors of wel-come, bring-ing Good News un-to all,
join-ing hands to work as proph-ets, break-ing down op-pres-sion's wall.

3. Sis-ter-Broth-er Spir-it gives us guid-ance for com-mu-ni-ty,
help-ing us to grow to-geth-er, find-ing all we're meant to be.
Var-ied gifts, re-ceived and val-ued, join to bring new life to birth,
streams of beau-ty, peace, and jus-tice flow-ing free-ly through the earth.

Words: Jann Aldredge-Clanton
Music: Ludwig van Beethoven
Words © 2007 Jann Aldredge-Clanton.

HYMN TO JOY
8.7.8.7 D

Community, Vision

22 We Come to Tell Our Stories

Revelation 21:5

1. We come to tell our stories, our sacred truth impart;
O Sister-Brother Spirit, inspire our minds and hearts.
We weave our lives with stories; a tapestry unfolds,

2. O Sister-Brother Spirit, within us and above,
revealing through our stories Your everlasting love,
empower us through our stories to claim our voices strong,

3. O Sister-Brother Spirit, we hear Your gentle call
to share our sacred stories, that liberate us all.
Our stories join together to show a wider view,

Words: Jann Aldredge-Clanton
Music: William G. Fischer
Words © 2009 Jann Aldredge-Clanton

HANKEY
7.6.7.6 D with refrain

Call, Social Justice

23   Wisdom Calls Us to Her Mission
Proverbs 8:20; James 3:13-18

1. Wis-dom calls us to Her mis-sion, bring-ing peace to all the earth;
2. Wis-dom leads on paths of jus-tice, teach-ing peo-ple to be fair;
3. Ho-ly Wis-dom guides us dai-ly on the jour-ney of our lives,

as we fol-low Wis-dom's guid-ance, love-ly works we bring to birth.
when we fol-low Wis-dom's guid-ance, we will show Her ten-der care.
giv-ing strength for do-ing jus-tice, speak-ing truth, and end-ing strife.

Wis-dom gives us deep-est bless-ings, fills our lives with gen-tle-ness;
O-ver-com-ing greed and en-vy, Wis-dom gives us o-pen hearts;
Joined with Wis-dom we will blos-som, bear-ing fruits of love and peace;

we can join in Wis-dom's ac-tions, show-ing forth Her right-eous-ness.
with Her Spir-it liv-ing in us, lov-ing kind-ness we im-part.
with Her pure and gen-tle Spir-it, all our gifts we now re-lease.

Words: Jann Aldredge-Clanton
Music: attr. B.F. White; arr. Larry E. Schultz

BEACH SPRING
8.7.8.7 D

Words © 2009 Jann Aldredge-Clanton; Music arr. © 2011 Larry E. Schultz.

Call, Creativity

Ruah,* the Spirit, Gives Each One a Song 24
Psalm 96:1, 144:9; Isaiah 30:29

1. Ru-ah, the Spirit, gives each one a song;
   in Her creative world we all belong.
   Beauty and grace dwell deep within each heart;
   in new creation everyone takes part.

2. Ru-ah, the Spirit, gives each one a song,
   healing our world and overcoming wrong.
   Now our creative work we bring to birth,
   singing through night and day for peace on earth.

3. Ru-ah, the Spirit, gives each one a song,
   sharing our talents, voices growing strong.
   Joining together, we shall sing as one,
   with visions of our work of justice done.

Words: Jann Aldredge-Clanton
Music: Frederick C. Atkinson
Words © 2008 Jann Aldredge-Clanton.

MORECAMBE
10.10.10.10
*Ruah is the word for "Spirit" in the Hebrew Scriptures.

Mission, Vision

25 Come Now, and Follow Wisdom

Proverbs 1:20-25, 3:13-18; James 3:17

1. Come now, and follow Wisdom on healing paths of peace;
She calls us to move forward to help all violence cease.
Oh why don't people listen and follow Wisdom's way?
So many still ignore Her, refusing Her new day.

2. With Wisdom we discover our mission on this earth;
we find our deepest purpose and new creation birth.
New challenges and visions engage our fullest gifts;
we find our true fulfillment as others we uplift.

3. The radiant light of Wisdom down through the ages beams;
She guides us to recover our highest hopes and dreams.
With Wisdom we find power to change the world each day,
to free ourselves and others to live the fairest way.

Words: Jann Aldredge-Clanton
Music: Samuel S. Wesley

AURELIA
7.6.7.6 D

Words © 2009 Jann Aldredge-Clanton.

Creation, Call

Midwife Divine Is Bringing Life to Birth   26
Psalm 22:9-10

1. Mid-wife Di-vine is bring-ing life to birth; She calls forth beau-ty ev-ery night and day. With gen-tle power She moves through-out the earth, and o-pens paths to new cre-a-tive ways; She gives Her help to all who la-bor long, and calms our fears with ten-der birth-ing songs.

2. Mid-wife Di-vine is call-ing deep with-in, through Ho-ly Dark-ness guid-ing all the way; She gives us hope new ven-tures to be-gin; Her lov-ing care for-ev-er with us stays. She gives us vi-sions of a world re-born; with Her we la-bor for a peace-ful morn.

Words: Jann Aldredge-Clanton
Music: Jean Sibelius; arr. Larry E. Schultz

FINLANDIA
10.10.10.10.10.10

Words © 2011 Jann Aldredge-Clanton. Music arr. © 2006 Larry E. Schultz

Call, Mission

27 Wisdom Graciously Gives to All
Proverbs 1:20-23, 3:13-18

1. Wis-dom gra-cious-ly gives to all won-der-ful words of life;
2. Sing them o-ver a-gain to me, won-der-ful words of life;
3. Sweet-ly ech-o *So-phi-a's call, won-der-ful words of life;

lis-ten now to Her lov-ing call, won-der-ful words of life;
let me more of their beau-ty see, won-der-ful words of life;
of-fer jus-tice and peace to all, won-der-ful words of life.

words so free-ly giv-en, mov-ing us to heav-en;
words of life and beau-ty, teach me faith and du-ty;
Wis-dom-Guide and Sav-ior, wor-ship now and for-ev-er;

Words: Philip P. Bliss; alt. Larry E. Schultz
Music: Philip P. Bliss

WORDS OF LIFE
Irregular

Alteration ©2010 Larry E. Schultz

*Greek word for "Wisdom," a feminine image of God.

beau-ti-ful words, won-der-ful words, won-der-ful words of life,

beau-ti-ful words, won-der-ful words, won-der-ful words of life.

Guidance, Care

28 Mother Eagle in the Sky
Deuteronomy 32:11-12

Bracketed measures may be played on **Bass Xylophone**.

1. Mother Eagle in the sky, teaching little birds to fly, help us all to stretch and grow; guide us all Your love to show.
2. Mother Eagle in the sky, teaching little birds to fly, help us all to learn each day; guide us in Your caring way.

Words: Jann Aldredge-Clanton
Music: Larry E. Schultz

ADAIR
7.7.7.7

Words © 2009 Jann Aldredge-Clanton; Music ©2009 Larry E. Schultz.
from *Sing and Dance and Play with Joy! Inclusive Songs for Young Children,* used in multigenerational settings.

Where Are You When We Need You?

Lament
29

Psalm 22:1-2, 44:23-25, 77:1-5

1. Where are You when we need You, O Maker of us all?
How can we know You see us and hear us when we call?
Do You not feel the suffering of people everywhere?
Why do You hide Your goodness, as though You do not care?

2. Why can't You stop the anguish; why can't You stop the pain?
Why don't You come to help us and ease the heavy strain?
How can we know You love us when we don't feel You near?
Will You come bring us comfort and take away our fear?

3. Rise up and come to help us; awake and hear our cries;
restore our souls and bodies; on You our hope relies.
We long to feel Your presence, our Sister-Brother-Friend;
come, bring Your loving kindness; Your healing power send.

Words: Jann Aldredge-Clanton
Music: Hans Leo Hassler; harm. Johann Sebastian Bach

PASSION CHORALE
7.6.7.6 D

Lament

30   How Long Will People Suffer?

Proverbs 1:20-24, 3:13-18; Matthew 23:37

1. How long will people suffer from violence and abuse?
   How long will Wisdom's healing ways be stifled and refused?
   How long will Wisdom cry out with Her words of love and peace?
   How long must Wisdom raise Her voice before our wars will cease?

2. How long must Wisdom cry out before injustice ends?
   How often through the prophets has She tried our world to mend?
   O why do people still reject Her liberating ways?
   O when will everyone unite to work for peaceful days?

3. Still Wisdom comes to help us in overcoming strife;
   She longs for all to follow Her on paths of truth and life.
   As partners let us join with Her in making peace on earth,
   restoring hope and taking part in new creation's birth.

Words: Jann Aldredge-Clanton
Music: Frederick C. Maker

ST. CHRISTOPHER
Irregular

Words © 2010 Jann Aldredge-Clanton.

Comfort, Hope

El Shaddai* Will Come to Help Us   31
Genesis 49:25; Isaiah 49:15, 66:13

1. El Shaddai will come to help us, hearing every painful plea;
   though the world around us rages, She will still our comfort be.
   Holding all in loving care, She will every burden bear.
2. Through the midst of pain and sorrow, El Shaddai will nurture all;
   She will come through swelling tempests, helping when we faint and fall.
   Blessings from Her womb and breasts bring all weary ones to rest.
3. El Shaddai with deep compassion will forever with us stay;
   giving guidance through each challenge, She will show the healing way.
   Helping all our fears release, She will lead to hope and peace.

Words: Jann Aldredge-Clanton
Music: Henry J. Gauntlett
Words © 2010 Jann Aldredge-Clanton.

IRBY
8.7.8.7.7.7

El Shaddai is a Hebrew name translated "God of the Breasts," "the Breasted God," or "God Almighty."

Healing, Comfort

32 Our Shepherd Gives Us All We Need
Psalm 23

1. Our Shepherd gives us all we need; She nurtures us each day. Through meadows green Her pathways lead to show the peaceful way.
2. When we are wounded and distressed, She takes us in Her arms; our Shepherd gives us healing rest and keeps us from alarm.
3. Our Shepherd feels our deepest grief; She comforts us through pain; from all our fears we find relief, our strength and hope regain.
4. Our Shepherd's gentle, loving care restores our souls each day. Her goodness flows forth everywhere, and with us always stays.

Words: Jann Aldredge-Clanton
Music: Jessie S. Irvine
Words © 2010 Jann Aldredge-Clanton.

CRIMOND
8.6.8.6 (CM)

Healing, Hope

34 Our Souls Find Rest and Comfort

Genesis 49:25; Isaiah 66:13

1. Our souls find rest and comfort, for El Shaddai* is near;
with tender care She holds us and takes away all fear.
No pain can overcome us; no storm can bring alarm,
for El Shaddai secures all within Her loving arms.

2. No struggle can defeat us; no grief can bring despair,
for El Shaddai will nurture all people everywhere.
She gently draws us closer and sings a healing song;
Her voice of reassurance goes with us all life long.

3. New hope springs up within us, for El Shaddai brings peace;
She gives all earth Her blessings, so justice will increase.
Now let all come together to show Her peaceful way,
so everyone will blossom to bring a bright new day.

Words: Jann Aldredge-Clanton
Music: Anonymous

Words © 2010 Jann Aldredge-Clanton.

WHITFIELD
7.6.7.6 D

El Shaddai is a Hebrew name translated "God of the Breasts," "the Breasted God," or "God Almighty."

Assurance, Eternal Life

Our Shepherd Comes in Loving Care 35
Psalm 23, 84

1. Our Shepherd comes in loving care; She nurtures us each day.
2. When we are weak, our Shepherd comes, and She restores our souls.
3. Through every valley filled with grief, our Shepherd calms our fears.
4. She makes a feast for everyone; Her blessings flow each day.

By waters still and meadows green She leads to peaceful ways.
She guides us all on healing paths and makes us fully whole.
In loving arms She comforts us and holds us always near.
And in Her lovely dwelling place forever we will stay.

Words: Jann Aldredge-Clanton
Music: James L. Bain; arr. Larry E. Schultz

BROTHER JAMES' AIR
8.6.8.6.8.6

Words © 2010 Jann Aldredge-Clanton; Music arr. © 2010 Larry E. Schultz

Peace, Comfort

36 Come, Christ-Sophia, Come

Matthew 11:28-30

1. Come, Christ-Sophia, come; ease pain and grief; daily we call to You, seeking relief. Help us our fears release; bring us Your healing peace; bring healing peace; bring healing peace.

2. Come to our wounded world, crying for care; come, Christ-Sophia, come, burdens to share. Help all the violence cease; bring us Your healing peace; bring healing peace; bring healing peace.

3. Come, Christ-Sophia, come, Your truth unfold; give us the strength to join Your mission bold. Help us Your love increase, working for healing peace; bring healing peace; bring healing peace.

Words: Jann Aldredge-Clanton
Music: William Howard Doane
Words © 2010 Jann Aldredge-Clanton.

MORE LOVE TO THEE
6.4.6.4.6.6.6.4.4

Dedication

O Loving Maker, Bless This Child, We Pray 37

Genesis 1:26-27; Proverbs 3:17; 2 Timothy 1:7

1. O Loving Maker, bless this child, we pray;
bless this new life among us here today,
in Your own image, wonderful and free,
as You created everyone to be.

2. O Holy Wisdom, in us and above,
guide us to nurture children with Your love,
that on Your peaceful pathways all may go,
making the world far better than we know.

3. O Holy Spirit, with us from our birth,
bless all the children everywhere on earth.
May all be well in body, mind, and soul,
growing with You: creative, loving, whole.

Words: Jann Aldredge-Clanton
Music: Edward J. Hopkins
Words © 2010 Jann Aldredge-Clanton.

ELLERS
10.10.10.10

Dedication

38 Great Creator, Bless This Child

Genesis 1:26-27; Ephesians 4:32

1. Great Cre-a-tor, bless this child, mir-a-cle You brought to birth.
2. Great Cre-a-tor, bless each child, in Your im-age made to be.
3. Great Cre-a-tor, Friend and Guide, bless all chil-dren ev-ery-where.

Here we cel-e-brate this child, liv-ing gift with us on earth.
Guide and nur-ture ev-ery child, grow-ing with Your Spir-it free.
May each one with You a-bide, learn-ing dai-ly how to share.

Help us all with You to grow, and Your lov-ing kind-ness show.

Words: Jann Aldredge-Clanton
Music: Conrad Kocher; adapt. William Henry Monk
Words © 2010 Jann Aldredge-Clanton.

DIX
7.7.7.7 with refrain

Celebration, Thanksgiving

O Holy One, We Sing Your Praise   39
Psalm 71:14-24

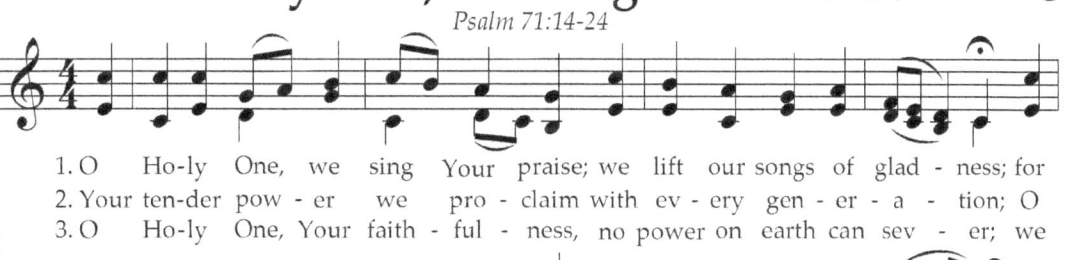

1. O Holy One, we sing Your praise; we lift our songs of gladness; for
2. Your tender power we proclaim with every generation; O
3. O Holy One, Your faithfulness, no power on earth can sever; we

You with hope our spirits raise; You comfort us in sadness. From
Holy One, Your gifts we claim with joy and celebration. Your
celebrate Your righteousness that sparks our best endeavor. The

youth to age we see Your acts that set us free; when all our strength has
wondrous deeds we sing; our gratitude we bring; Your loving care re-
highest heavens tell Your love that never fails; Your blessings all day

left, You lift us from the depths; we praise Your grace and goodness.
vives and keeps our hope alive; we give You adoration.
long inspire our greatest songs; we sing Your praise forever.

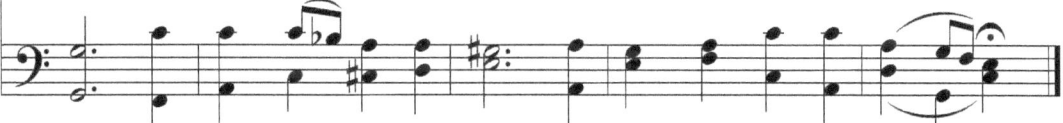

Words: Jann Aldredge-Clanton
Music: Martin Luther; arr. J.S. Bach
Words © 2009 Jann Aldredge-Clanton.

EIN' FESTE BURG
8.7.8.7.6.6.6.6.7

Thanksgiving, Creation

40   We Praise the Works of Wisdom

Psalm 104:1-30; Proverbs 3:13-15, 9:1, 5-6

1. We praise the works of Wis-dom, how man-i-fold and great;
She fills the earth with won-ders, more than we can re-late.
The flow-ing streams give nur-ture to crea-tures large and small,

2. The works of Wis-dom flour-ish through dark-ness and through light;
the chip-munks play in for-ests, and ea-gles soar in flight.
The sport-ing whales in o-ceans, all come from Wis-dom's hand;

3. We bring our thanks to Wis-dom for nour-ish-ing our lives;
Her bread and wine in-crease strength, our hearts and minds re-vive.
Re-joice in Wis-dom's glo-ry, Her ra-diant maj-es-ty;

Words: Jann Aldredge-Clanton   WIR PFLUGEN
Music: Johann A. P. Schulz   7.6.7.6 D with refrain
Words © 2009 Jann Aldredge-Clanton.

Praise, Creativity

Composer of All the Music We Hear   42

Psalm 33:1-3; 1 Corinthians 14:15

1. Com-pos-er of all the mu-sic we hear, of har-mo-nies rich and mel-o-dies clear, of rhy-thm that puls-es with tem-po and beat, Your mu-sic en-liv-ens our voic-es and feet.

2. Con-duc-tor of all the mu-sic we sing, Your ges-tures in-spire each of-fering we bring, of in-stru-ments gath-ered with voic-es in song. Your mu-sic en-folds us; to You we be-long.

3. Con-vey-or of all the mu-sic we feel, with pow-er to com-fort, strength-en and heal, in modes that ex-press deep e-mo-tion, we find Your mu-sic en-gag-es both spir-it and mind.

4. Mu-si-cian Di-vine, the gift of Your art en-rich-es the mind and bod-y and heart, en-light-ens our jour-ney through life with its sound. We praise You for mu-sic, Your gift most pro-found.

Words and Music: Larry E. Schultz
Words and Music © 2008 Larry E. Schultz.

TIMBERLAKE
10.10.11.11

*Soprano voices may sing cue-sized notes on Stanza 4.

Advent, Christmas

Holy Wisdom Comes to Earth

44

Proverbs 1:20-23, 3:13-18, 8:1-20; Matthew 23:37

1. Holy Wisdom comes to earth, calling through the ages; few have recognized Her birth; few have sung Her praises. Long have people failed to see Wisdom's peaceful pathway, long refused Her liberty, leading to a new day.
2. Holy Wisdom still draws near, paths of justice showing, sending prophets through the years, truth and kindness sowing. Holy Wisdom ends the strife, bringing transformation; She is like a Tree of Life, healing all creation.
3. Holy Wisdom sets us free, coming in Her glory; now Her Advent we can see; now we tell Her story. Holy Wisdom breaks down walls, bringing in new freedom; praise Her power in us all; praise the Queen of Wisdom.

Words: Jann Aldredge-Clanton
Music: *Piae Cantiones*; arr. Ernest MacMillan
Words © 2009 Jann Aldredge-Clanton.

TEMPUS ADEST FLORIDUM
7.6.7.6 D

Advent

45 Come to Our World, O Christ-Sophia

Proverbs 3:17-18; 1 Corinthians 1:24; 2 Corinthians 5:17; John 14:6

1. Come to our world, O Christ-Sophia, Wisdom; our hearts are longing for Your peaceful way. Lead us from fear and bondage into freedom; with You we labor to bring Your new day.
2. Transform our world, O Christ-Sophia, Wisdom; the poor and wounded await healing days. Give us the power to sound Your call to freedom; as equal partners, we show Your new way.
3. Led by Your Truth and Life within us growing, we follow You on Your pathways of peace. Filled with Your grace, Your loving kindness showing, we share our gifts and our visions release. Our weary world still longs for new creation, for peace and justice

Words: Jann Aldredge-Clanton
Music: Adolphe Adam
Words © 2008 Jann Aldredge-Clanton.

CANTIQUE DE NOEL
Irregular

Advent

46 Come to Free Us, Christ-Sophia

Proverbs 3:17; 1 Corinthians 1:24; 2 Corinthians 5:17

1. Come to free us, Christ-Sophia, through Your just and peaceful way;
for Your Advent we have waited, hoping for a better day.
Violence ending, conflict mending, nature tending, freedom sending:
Christ-Sophia, come today.

2. All are longing for belonging in a new community,
equal partners on a mission to bring love and harmony.
One another's burdens bearing, filled with caring, ventures daring:
Christ-Sophia, come today.

3. Come to free us, Christ-Sophia, bringing peace throughout the earth;
we become Your new creation, as we claim our sacred worth.
Fairness showing, beauty knowing, wisdom growing, kindness flowing:
Christ-Sophia, come today.

Words: Jann Aldredge-Clanton
Music: Polish carol; arr. Larry E. Schultz

W ZLOBIE LEZY
8.7.8.7.8.8.7

Words © 2009 Jann Aldredge-Clanton; Music arr. © 2011 Larry E. Schultz.

Christmas

48 Celebrate Sophia's* Birth
Proverbs 3:13-18

1. Cel-e-brate Sophia's birth, bringing healing to the earth;
Holy Wisdom opens hearts, peace and freedom She imparts.

2. Praise Sophia through the years, Holy Wisdom coming near,
born in Mary Magdalene, born in Mother Mary, Queen.

3. Praise Sophia, Tree of Life, blooming forth to end the strife;
She brings gifts beyond compare, stirring us to dream and dare.

Refrain: Gloria, blessed be Sophia! Gloria, blessed be Sophia!

Words: Jann Aldredge-Clanton
Music: French carol; arr. Warren M. Angell
Words © 2009 Jann Aldredge-Clanton.

GLORIA
7.7.7.7 with refrain

*Sophia is the Greek word for "Wisdom," linked to Christ in the Christian Scriptures.

Christmas

Sing of Peace, Holy Peace

49

Proverbs 3:13-17; 2 Corinthians 5:17

1. Sing of peace, ho - ly peace; sing of all gifts re - leased.
2. Sing of peace, ho - ly peace. When will all vio - lence cease?
3. Sing of peace, ho - ly peace; hope and joy now in - crease.

As we work for peace on earth, new cre - a - tion comes to birth;
Through our jus - tice work each day, Wis-dom comes to show the way;
Through our works of love each day, Ho - ly Wis - dom comes to stay;

Christ - So - phi - a is born; Christ - So - phi - a is born.
Christ - So - phi - a is born; Christ - So - phi - a is born.
Christ - So - phi - a is born; Christ - So - phi - a is born.

Words: Jann Aldredge-Clanton
Music: Franz Gruber

STILLE NACHT
Irregular

Words © 2009 Jann Aldredge-Clanton.

Epiphany

50 Star of Wonder, Star of Wisdom

Proverbs 3:17-18

1. Star of Wonder, Star of Wisdom, guide us to find Your way;
shine upon us with Your vision of bright and peaceful days.
Lead us forward through each challenge, helping all be fair and free,

2. Star of Wonder, Star of Wisdom, illumine minds and hearts;
guide us on Your healing mission; Your radiant life impart.
Light new pathways for our journey, leading to creation new;

Words: Jann Aldredge-Clanton
Music: Gustav Holst
Words © 2009 Jann Aldredge-Clanton.

THAXTED
14.14.15.14.14.14

Epiphany

51 Ancient Wisdom, Mother of Earth

Proverbs 3:13-18, 8:23-31

1. Ancient Wisdom, Mother of earth, bringing all creation to birth, with Her power, we will flower, feeling our sacred worth.
2. Black Madonna, Mother of all, loving us whatever befalls, always guiding and abiding, within our hearts She calls.
3. Guadalupe, our Lady and Queen, from Her holy treasures we glean; She is healing and revealing more than we've ever seen.

O now return to Her for peace; hope and justice will increase. Re-creating, liberating, She will all our dreams release.

Words: Jann Aldredge-Clanton
Music: John Henry Hopkins, Jr.
Words © 2010 Jann Aldredge-Clanton.

KINGS OF ORIENT
8.8.8.6 with refrain

Creation, Epiphany

O Holy Darkness, Source of Life   52

Genesis 1; Isaiah 45:3; Psalm 139:11-12

1. O Holy Darkness, Source of Life, Your blessings flow throughout the earth; Your beauty stirs us all to strive with You creation to revive, and bring Your seeds to birth.
2. Creative Darkness, Faithful Guide, we hear Your music in our souls; Your treasures open deep and wide, as in Your center we abide, and grow more fully whole.
3. O Holy Darkness, Loving Friend, Your grace restores us night and day; we join together as we tend Your world of goodness without end, and find Your peaceful way.

Words: Jann Aldredge-Clanton
Music: Albert L. Peace
Words © 2010 Jann Aldredge-Clanton.

ST. MARGARET
8.8.8.8.6

Resurrection, Hope

53 We Are an Easter People

John 15:13, 1:1; Matthew 28:20, 25:40; 1 Corinthians 1:24

1. We are an Easter people; we celebrate new life;
   we share an Easter mission of healing pain and strife.
   We welcome new creation, unfolding every day;
   our risen Friend-Companion shows us the peaceful way.

2. We are an Easter people; we sing an Easter song;
   new hope springs up each morning to help us labor long.
   Our risen Brother-Sister goes with us every day
   to join the poor and hungry and show the healing way.

3. We are an Easter people; our gifts can fully flower;
   the Wisdom-Word within us has given us new power.
   Our resurrection story inspires our highest dreams;
   our resurrection vision before us brightly beams.

Words: Jann Aldredge-Clanton
Music: Henry T. Smart
Words © 2009 Jann Aldredge-Clanton.

LANCASHIRE
7.6.7.6 D

Power, Hope

Come, Easter People, Come, Rejoice 54

Matthew 25:40; Proverbs 3:17

1. Come, Easter people, come, rejoice; celebrate life; lift up each voice. Our risen Sister-Brother-Friend gives us new power, our world to mend.
2. Sing, Easter people, sing of life; dream of a world that's free of strife. Wisdom within us guides the way to make our dreams come true some day.
3. Go, Easter people, go in peace throughout the world, our gifts release. Our risen Sister-Brother-Friend goes with us all, new hope to send.

Words: Jann Aldredge-Clanton
Music: John Hatton
Words © 2009 Jann Aldredge-Clanton.

DUKE STREET
8.8.8.8 (LM)

Pentecost

55 Ruah,* Spirit, Come Today
Genesis 1:1-2; Acts 2:1-18

1. Ruah, Spirit, come today, as You've come through ages past, changing all who seek Your way, giving hope for peace at last. Help us claim this
2. Ruah, Spirit, Breath of Life, giving birth to all we know, move in us, our souls revive with Your everlasting flow. Stir our hearts with
3. Ruah, Spirit, bold and free, forming and reforming all, re-create communities by Your liberating call. Sons and daughters

Words: Jann Aldredge-Clanton
Music: Joseph Parry
Words © 2010 Jann Aldredge-Clanton.

ABERYSTWYTH
7.7.7.7 D

Ruah is the word for "Spirit" in the Hebrew Scriptures.

Pentecost

56 Waiting Now with Expectation
Acts 2:1-18; Galatians 5:22-23

1. Wait-ing now with ex-pec-ta-tion, seek-ing hope for peace on earth,
2. Dar-ing Spir-it, liv-ing in us, help us join Your mis-sion bold;
3. Lov-ing, Ev-er-last-ing Spir-it, deep with-in and all a-round,

we are long-ing, Ho-ly Spir-it, for Your power that brings re-birth.
give us cour-age for each chal-lenge, pa-tience as Your plan un-folds.
guide us on cre-a-tive ven-tures, so our tal-ents will a-bound.

Send Your Pen-te-cos-tal bless-ings, might-y wind, trans-form-ing fire,
Break-ing down op-pres-sive sys-tems, we u-nite to end the strife,
Gifts and grac-es o-ver-flow-ing show Your beau-ty ev-ery-where,

stir-ring all to lov-ing kind-ness, as new vi-sions You in-spire.
part-ners in Your work of jus-tice, bring-ing lib-er-at-ing life.
all cre-a-tion joined to-geth-er, filled with joy be-yond com-pare.

Words: Jann Aldredge-Clanton
Music: Rowland H. Prichard
Words © 2010 Jann Aldredge-Clanton.

HYFRYDOL
8.7.8.7 D

NOTES

1, 1a.   O Loving Creator, We Labor with You
20.   Celebrate Our Life Together

The twelfth international contest for hymn writers sponsored by the Macalester Plymouth United Church of St. Paul, Minnesota, in 2007, invited "new texts to use on Mother's Day, sensitive to the changing nature of family life, and affirming feminist calls for equality." These topics attracted me because of my years of writing and speaking on feminist theology and inclusive divine imagery in worship as vital to equality. I submitted these two hymns to the contest, and "O Loving Creator," written to the tune ST. DENIO, won honorable mention. Later that year Rev. Larry E. Schultz composed a new tune, VESTA, for this hymn. This flowing and majestic tune enhances the image of the Creator as both tender and strong. Larry named this tune in memory of his maternal grandmother, Erma Vesta Yarbrough.

2.   Sister-Brother, Peaceful Spirit

This hymn and others in *Inclusive Hymns for Liberation, Peace, and Justice* pair Sister and Brother images to symbolize partnership in human relationships and partnership with the Divine. Sister-Brother Divine images suggest mutuality more than do parental images. This hymn also celebrates and is dedicated to the strong women in my family who have worked to make "all be fair and free": my mother, Eva; sister, Anne; daughter-in-law, Beth; niece, DeAnne. The hymn is also dedicated to my sons, Chad and Brett; husband, David; and nephew, David, in celebration of their strong brotherly love that contributes to "building bridges."

3.   Praise Wisdom in Our Hearts
23. Wisdom Calls Us to Her Mission

In September of 2009 at Church in the Cliff in Dallas, Texas, Pastor Courtney Pinkerton led a discussion based on James 3:13-18. This passage describes Divine Wisdom as peaceful, gentle, fair, caring, generous, and truthful. I went home and wrote "Wisdom Calls Us to Her Mission." About a month earlier, our congregation sang "Come, Christians, Join to Sing." This lively tune played over and over in my mind, inspiring me to write "Praise Wisdom in Our Hearts" to this music. I also wrote these hymns in gratitude to Rev. Dr. Nancy Ellett Allison, who founded CityChurch, now called Church in the Cliff. I am grateful to CityChurch/Church in the Cliff for affirming my hymn writing and for often singing my hymns in worship services.

6.   Arise and Celebrate

The inspiration for this hymn came from the book *All We're Meant to Be: A Biblical Approach to Women's Liberation*, by Letha Dawson Scanzoni and Nancy A. Hardesty (Word Inc., 1974). This was the first book I read that gave biblical support for the equality of women and men in the home and the church. *All We're Meant to Be* also expanded my images of the Divine to include more than male. This book is now in its third edition: Letha Dawson Scanzoni and Nancy A. Hardesty, *All We're Meant to Be: Biblical Feminism for Today* (Eerdmans, 1992).

9.   Shekhinah Is Our Dwelling Place

Revs. Marcia Fleischman and Paul Smith, co-pastors of Broadway Church in Kansas City, inspired this hymn. They have written and taught extensively on "our divinity," the "life Divine within us all" (Fleischman, *Wild Woman Theology: In the Arms of Loving Mother God*, AuthorHouse, 2009; Smith, *Integral Christianity: The Spirit's Call to Evolve*, Paragon House, 2011). They are among the ministers featured in my book, *Changing Church: Stories of Liberating Ministers* (Cascade Books, 2011).

10. Celebrate the Works of Wisdom

In the fall of 2009, Perkins School of Theology launched "Wisdom Works at Perkins" with the purpose of exploring the possibilities of Divine Wisdom for guidance on works of liberation, justice, and radical equality. This program focuses on creating emancipatory groups as described by Dr. Marjorie Procter-Smith in her book *The Church in Her House* (Pilgrim Press, 2008). According to Procter-Smith "emancipatory" means freedom of all people, recognizing the interrelationship of multiple forms of oppression. Another Perkins professor, Rev. Dr. Isabel Docampo, and I envisioned the "Wisdom Works at Perkins" program to include creative works of art, music, poetry, and prose by students and faculty for use in Perkins Chapel services, appropriate places around campus, and/or Perkins' publications. I wrote "Celebrate the Works of Wisdom" for this program. The hymn and the title of the program play on the word "works" as a noun and a verb. Rev. Dr. Docampo is among the ministers featured in my book, *Changing Church: Stories of Liberating Ministers* (Cascade Books, 2011).

11. Wisdom, Sophia, Joins in Our Labor

Written for the 2008 Faith and Feminism/Womanist/Mujerista Conference in San Francisco, this hymn reflects the process theology of the keynote speaker, Dr. Carol Christ, author of *She Who Changes: Re-Imagining the Divine in the World* (Palgrave Macmillan, 2003).

13. The Music Is Ringing
50. Star of Wonder, Star of Wisdom

Rev. Larry Schultz inspired these hymns as he talked about string theory in physics and envisioned new possibilities for music ministry from this theory of all the particles of life as vibrating strings. He pondered, "If we discovered what it means for us all to be musical beings, vibrating sound waves, how would that connect us with the universe?" The images of the universe vibrating and singing "with all creatures on earth" came to me, and I wrote "The Music Is Ringing" to the lilting tune ASH GROVE. I wrote "Star of Wonder, Star of Wisdom" to the majestic tune THAXTED, which also seemed appropriate to convey the theme of the whole universe opening with possibility. Rev. Schultz is among the ministers featured in my book, *Changing Church: Stories of Liberating Ministers* (Cascade Books, 2011).

The expansive theology in these two hymns and many others in this collection make them appropriate for interfaith celebrations and worship services.

14. Creation Calls to Us for Help
15. Our Mother-Father, Friend and Source

It was a joy to collaborate with Larry E. Schultz on "We Thank You, God, for Animal Friends" (Choristers Guild, 2007), an anthem that names a variety of animals and ends with a "promise to care for animals everywhere." Along with many hymns in *Inclusive Hymns for Liberating Christians* (e.g. #48, 52, 77, 114, 115), "Creation Calls to Us for Help" and "Our Mother-Father, Friend and Source" continue my celebration of creation and my desire to contribute to caring for the environment. I draw from the catalog of animals in Psalm 104 and from experiencing my grandchildren's delight over animals at the zoo and in parks.

17. We Long to Dwell in Unity

This hymn comes from my experience as director of the Waco Conference of Christians and Jews, now called the Greater Waco Interfaith Conference, and as chair of the Interfaith Task Force at Baylor University Medical Center in Dallas. More and more I have come to see the need for cooperation and dialog among faith groups. Another influence on this hymn is Deborah Harris' "A Psalm of Unity," sung at an annual banquet of the Waco Conference of Christians and Jews and included in my children's book, *God, A Word for Girls and Boys* (Glad River Publications, 1993; Wipf & Stock Publishers, 2007).

18. Sacred Darkness Dwelling
52. O Holy Darkness, Source of Life

These hymns continue my reclaiming of darkness as a positive image in worship. (See *Inclusive Hymns for Liberating Christians*, #48, 90, 99.) In many hymns and litanies light carries positive meanings, and darkness carries negative connotations. "Sacred Darkness Dwelling" images darkness as the creative miracle within each person and all life. "O Holy Darkness, Source of Life" images darkness as sacred Source, Guide, and Friend, bringing treasures of beauty and grace to restore all creation.

19. We Praise You, Holy Other

This hymn is written in gratitude for the prophetic ministry of Rev. Stacy Boorn, pastor of Ebenezer/herchurch Lutheran. In her preaching and teaching, Rev. Boorn often refers to Deity as "Holy Other," an image that includes all those who are made to feel "other" because of sexual orientation, gender, race, class, and/or disability. Rev. Boorn is among the ministers featured in my book, *Changing Church: Stories of Liberating Ministers* (Cascade Books, 2011).

Rev. Larry E. Schultz wrote a vibrant new arrangement for the traditional hymn tune NYLAND. This tune arrangement is lovingly dedicated to Larry's wife, Cindy, whose expressive gifts as a pianist and church organist inspire and inform his composing and arranging.

22. We Come to Tell Our Stories

This hymn, inspired by New Wineskins Community, celebrates the sacred power of stories. This inclusive, ecumenical worship Community gives equal value to every person's voice and encourages the sharing of our stories. The name "New Wineskins," coming from the metaphor in Matthew 9:17, describes our search for new language and symbols to proclaim the gospel of liberation and shalom. The Community's worship includes female and male divine names and images, like "Sister-Brother Spirit" in "We Come to Tell our Stories," to support the equal value of all and to symbolize our shared power and responsibility. I wrote this hymn and others in this collection with gratitude to New Wineskins Community for encouraging my creation of hymns and for singing them with enthusiasm in our worship services.

24. Ruah, the Spirit, Gives Each One a Song

This hymn is inspired by a Native American Proverb: "The Great Spirit gave us each a song." My husband, David, gave me a framed copy of this Proverb, which I keep on my desk as I am writing. This hymn is dedicated to David in gratitude for his support of this new hymn collection and for his many gifts that have blessed my life and work.

28. Mother Eagle in the Sky
43. Ruah, Creator, Gave Birth to Us All

Larry E. Schultz and I wrote these two pieces originally for *Sing and Dance and Play with Joy! Inclusive Songs for Young Children* (Lulu, 2009). We created this book of songs and activities because we have seen how powerful *Imagine God! A Children's Musical Exploring and Expressing Images of God* (Choristers Guild, 2004) has been in teaching school-age girls and boys that they are all created in the divine image; we wanted to extend this inclusive theology to preschool children. In October of 2009, Larry and I led a multigenerational premier of the preschool songbook at Pullen Memorial Baptist Church in Raleigh, North Carolina. When I heard people of all ages singing these songs with great enthusiasm, I decided to include two of them in *Inclusive Hymns for Liberation, Peace, and Justice.* Bringing people of all ages together through inclusive worship music contributes to a vital faith community.

Larry chose the name ADAIR for the tune to "Mother Eagle in the Sky." He named this tune in memory of Margaret Adair, a Cherokee and "second mother" to him. In public school and church settings Margaret was a teacher and mentor to children, sharing her culture and faith. The Native American sound of this song highlights the connection with this tradition that reveres the eagle. In many Native American cultures, the eagle is a sacred bird, central to religious and spiritual customs. And in the scripture reference with this song, Deuteronomy 32:11-12, Mother Eagle is an image of the Divine.

29. Where Are You When We Need You?
30. How Long Will People Suffer?

Positive responses to "Are You Good and Are You Strong?" (hymn version #61 in *Inclusive Hymns for Liberating Christians*, Eakin Press, 2006; anthem version, Alfred Publishing Co., 2008) convinced me of the need to sing our questions as well as our praise in worship. Most worship services give little opportunity for lament, although the Psalms are filled with laments. These two hymns question our Maker about the suffering we experience and about all the violence and suffering in the world.

31. El Shaddai Will Come to Help Us
34. Our Souls Find Rest and Comfort

The inspiration for these two hymns came from Rev. Stacy Boorn and Ebenezer/herchurch Lutheran in San Francisco. Rev. Boorn asked me to write new lyrics to one of her favorite hymn tunes, IRBY (tune for "Once in Royal David's City").

She had also told me that one of the female divine names that Ebenezer Lutheran members love is *Shaddai*, meaning "the Breasted One," or "most High," because the church is in the shadow of what are called the "twin peaks" of San Francisco, that from a distance look like breasts. So they look out from the church and say, "There She is, *Shaddai*, right over there!" The comforting, nurturing images came also from Isaiah 49:15, Isaiah 66:13, and Genesis 49:25.

32. Our Shepherd Gives Us All We Need
35. Our Shepherd Comes in Loving Care

Shortly after the first edition of *In Whose Image? God and Gender* (Crossroad, 1990; 2nd edition, 2001) came out, my husband, David, gave me a recording of Bobby McFerrin's "The 23rd Psalm." McFerrin refers to the Shepherd as "She" throughout his song, illuminating the comforting and empowering images of the psalm in fresh ways. Convinced of the need for more female images of the tender Shepherd, along with the male images, I wrote these two hymns.

33. Come, Sophia, to Calm Our Souls

During the stress of a major vocational decision, I wrote this hymn to express my longing for *Sophia* Wisdom's guidance and peace. My hope is that it will be as helpful to others as it has become for me in my meditation and prayer life. This hymn calms me and often lulls me to sleep at night.

37. O Loving Maker, Bless This Child, We Pray
38. Great Creator, Bless This Child

These two hymns are dedicated to my grandsons: Paul, Emmett, and Lyle.

42. Composer of All the Music We Hear

Larry E. Schultz wrote both this hymn text and tune (TIMBERLAKE) in honor of his college music theory professor, Kathryne Timberlake, as a gift on her 85th birthday. This hymn prayer celebrates the Musician Divine's gift of music known in the foundational sounds and systems of melody, harmony, and rhythm; in music's ability to gather instruments and voices together; in its mysterious power to comfort, heal, and express deep emotion; and in its enrichment of mind, body, soul, and strength throughout life.

44. Holy Wisdom Comes to Earth
45. Come to Our World, O Christ-Sophia
46. Come to Free Us, Christ-Sophia
47. Come, Celebrate and Sing
48. Celebrate Sophia's Birth
49. Sing of Peace, Holy Peace

In 2009 Stacy Boorn, pastor of Ebenezer/herchurch Lutheran in San Francisco, and Steve Rausch, the minister of music, commissioned new hymns for Advent and Christmas. I was delighted because I had been called to hymn writing during the Advent season of 1994, when I had become especially aware of the exclusively masculine language in traditional Christmas carols. My deep gratitude goes to Rev. Stacy Boorn and Ebenezer/herchurch Lutheran for inspiring these hymns and many others in this collection. Exclusive language continues to predominate in Christmas songs, so I jumped at this invitation to write lyrics to additional familiar Christmas tunes (See others in *Inclusive Hymns for Liberating Christians*, e.g. #92-99).

"Holy Wisdom Comes to Earth" is dedicated to Kelly Schultz. From the time she was a young girl, Kelly has celebrated the image of Divine Wisdom as a "Tree of Life." When she was only three years old and heard the musical setting of *Old Turtle* (text by Douglas Wood), she immediately identified with this line referring to the Divine: "She is a great Tree!" Kelly responded, "That's my part!" Kelly is currently active in the youth group of Pullen Memorial Baptist Church, Raleigh, North Carolina, where she also sings in the youth choir and plays violin and percussion in the orchestra.

"Celebrate Sophia's Birth," also written for the 2009 Faith and Feminism/

Womanist/Mujerista Conference, sponsored by Ebenezer/herchurch, honors the work of the conference keynote speakers, China Galland and Margaret Starbird (Galland, *Longing for Darkness: Tara and the Black Madonna*, Penguin, 2007; Starbird, *The Woman with the Alabaster Jar: Mary Magdalen and the Holy Grail*, Bear and Company, 1993).

The lyrics of these Advent and Christmas hymns focus on the image of Wisdom (*Hokmah* in the Hebrew Scriptures and *Sophia* in the Greek language of the Christian Scriptures) and Christ-Sophia, drawn from the biblical parallel between Jesus Christ and Wisdom. My books, *In Search of the Christ-Sophia: An Inclusive Christology for Liberating Christians* (Twenty-Third Publications, 1995; Eakin Press, 2004) and *Praying with Christ-Sophia: Services for Healing and Renewal* (Twenty-Third Publications, 1996; Wipf & Stock Publishers, 2007), give biblical, historical, and theological explanation of this parallel, along with worship resources. These books on Christ-Sophia and books on other inclusive divine images are also available on www.jannaldredgeclanton.com.

53. We Are an Easter People
54. Come, Easter People, Come, Rejoice

These two hymns are dedicated to Ryan Schultz, who was baptized on Easter Sunday, April 12, 2009, at Pullen Memorial Baptist Church, Raleigh, North Carolina. Ryan is active in the church youth group, sings in the youth choir, and plays trumpet in the church orchestra.

TOPICAL INDEX OF HYMNS

ADVENT

Come to Free Us, Christ-Sophia 46
Come to Our World, O Christ-Sophia 45
Holy Wisdom Comes to Earth 44

ADVERSITY

El Shaddai Will Come to Help Us 31
Our Shepherd Comes in Loving Care 35
Our Shepherd Gives Us All We Need 32
Our Souls Find Rest and Comfort 34

ASSURANCE

El Shaddai Will Come to Help Us 31
Our Shepherd Comes in Loving Care 35
Our Shepherd Gives Us All We Need 32
Our Souls Find Rest and Comfort 34

BEAUTY

All the World with Beauty Shines 16
Celebrate the Works of Wisdom 10
Come to Free Us, Christ-Sophia 46

O Holy Darkness, Source of Life 52
Ruah, the Spirit, Gives Each One a Song 24
Star of Wonder, Star of Wisdom 50
The Music Is Ringing 13
Waiting Now with Expectation 56
We Praise the Works of Wisdom 40
Wisdom Graciously Gives to All 27
Wisdom, Sophia, Joins in Our Labor 11

CALL

Awake to Work for Peace on Earth 7
Come Now, and Follow Wisdom 25
Midwife Divine Is Bringing Life to Birth 26
Mother Eagle in the Sky 28
O Loving Creator, We Labor with You 1,1a
Ruah, the Spirit, Gives Each One a Song 24
Sister-Brother, Peaceful Spirit 2
We Long to Dwell in Unity 17
Wisdom Calls Us to Her Mission 23
Wisdom Graciously Gives to All 27

CARE OF CREATION (see also Earth Day)

All the World with Beauty Shines 16
Creation Calls to Us for Help 14
Our Mother-Father, Friend and Source 15
Sister-Brother, Peaceful Spirit 2
The Music Is Ringing 13

CARING FOR OTHERS

Come Now, and Follow Wisdom 25
Come to Free Us, Christ-Sophia 46
Mother Eagle in the Sky 28
O Loving Creator, We Labor with You 1,1a
We Are an Easter People 53
We Come to Tell Our Stories 22
When Will Justice Flow Like Waters? 8

CELEBRATION (see also Praise)

All the World with Beauty Shines 16
Celebrate Our Life Together 20
Celebrate Sophia's Birth 48
Celebrate the Good Creation 41
Celebrate the Works of Wisdom 10
Come, Celebrate and Sing 47
Great Creator, Bless This Child 38
O Holy One, We Sing Your Praise 39
We Are an Easter People 53

CHALLENGE

Come Now, and Follow Wisdom 25
El Shaddai Will Come to Help Us 31
Sister-Brother, Peaceful Spirit 2
Star of Wonder, Star of Wisdom 50

CHRISTMAS

Ancient Wisdom, Mother of Earth 51
Celebrate Sophia's Birth 48
Come, Celebrate and Sing 47
Holy Wisdom Comes to Earth 44
Sing of Peace, Holy Peace 49

COMFORT

Come, Christ-Sophia, Come 36
Come, Sophia, to Calm Our Souls 33
Composer of All the Music We Hear 42
El Shaddai Will Come to Help Us 31
Midwife Divine Is Bringing Life to Birth 26
O Holy One, We Sing Your Praise 39
Our Shepherd Comes in Loving Care 35
Our Shepherd Gives Us All We Need 32
Our Souls Find Rest and Comfort 34
Where Are You When We Need You? 29

COMMUNION

Celebrate Our Life Together 20
Sister-Brother, Peaceful Spirit 2
We Long to Dwell in Unity 17

COMMUNITY

Celebrate Our Life Together 20
Come to Free Us, Christ-Sophia 46
We Come to Tell Our Stories 22
We Gather Here to Pray 21

COURAGE

Sister-Brother, Peaceful Spirit 2
When Will Justice Flow Like Waters? 8
Waiting Now with Expectation 56
Wisdom Calls Us to Her Mission 23

COVENANT

Awake to Work for Peace on Earth 7
Behold Shekhinah Leading 5
Celebrate Our Life Together 20
Creation Calls to Us for Help 14
O Loving Creator, We Labor with You 1,1a
Sister-Brother, Peaceful Spirit 2
Wisdom Calls Us to Her Mission 23

CREATION

Ancient Wisdom, Mother of Earth 51
Behold Shekhinah Leading 5
Holy Wisdom Comes to Earth 44
Midwife Divine Is Bringing Life to Birth 26
O Holy Darkness, Source of Life 52
Our Mother-Father, Friend and Source 15
Ruah, Creator, Gave Birth to Us All 43
Ruah, Spirit, Come Today 55
Ruah, the Spirit-Source of All 4

Sacred Darkness Dwelling 18
Star of Wonder, Star of Wisdom 50
We Come to Tell Our Stories 22
We Praise the Works of Wisdom 40
When Will Justice Flow Like Waters? 8

CREATIVITY

Behold Shekhinah Leading 5
Composer of All the Music We Hear 42
O Holy Darkness, Source of Life 52
Ruah, the Spirit, Gives Each One a Song 24
Ruah, the Spirit-Source of All 4
Star of Wonder, Star of Wisdom 50
Wisdom Calls Us to Her Mission 23
Wisdom, Sophia, Joins in Our Labor 11

DEDICATION—CHILDREN

Great Creator, Bless This Child 38
O Loving Maker, Bless This Child, We Pray 37

DIVERSITY (see Unity and Diversity)

DIVINE IMAGES

Ancient Wisdom
    Ancient Wisdom, Mother of Earth 51
Black Madonna
    Ancient Wisdom, Mother of Earth 51
Breath of Life
    Ruah, Spirit, Come Today 55
Brother-Sister
    Sister-Brother, Peaceful Spirit 2
    We Are an Easter People 53
Brother-Sister Spirit
    We Long to Dwell in Unity 17
Christ-Sophia
    Arise and Celebrate 6
    Come, Christ-Sophia, Come 36
    Come to Free Us, Christ-Sophia 46

    Come to Our World, O Christ-Sophia 45
    Sing of Peace, Holy Peace 49

Composer
    Composer of All the Music We Hear 42

Conductor
    Composer of All the Music We Hear 42

Conveyor
    Composer of All the Music We Hear 42

Creative Darkness
    O Holy Darkness, Source of Life 52

Creative Love
    We Gather Here to Pray 21

Creating Spirit
    Creation Calls to Us for Help 14

Creative Spirit
    Our Mother-Father, Friend and Source 15
    We Gather Here to Pray 21

Creator
    Great Creator, Bless This Child 38
    O Loving Creator, We Labor with You 1,1a
    Ruah, Creator, Gave Birth to Us All 43

Daring Spirit
    Waiting Now with Expectation 56

El Shaddai
    El Shaddai Will Come to Help Us 31
    Our Souls Find Rest and Comfort 34

Everlasting Spirit
    Waiting Now with Expectation 56

Faithful Friend
    We Gather Here to Pray 21

Faithful Guide
    O Holy Darkness, Source of Life 52

Father-Mother Love
    Celebrate Our Life Together 20

Friend
    Great Creator, Bless This Child 38
    Our Mother-Father, Friend and Source 15

Friend-Companion
    We Are an Easter People 53

Guadalupe
    Ancient Wisdom, Mother of Earth 51

Guide
　Great Creator, Bless This Child 38
Holy Darkness
　Midwife Divine Is Bringing Life to Birth 26
　O Holy Darkness, Source of Life 52
Holy One
　O Holy One, We Sing Your Praise 39
Holy Other
　We Praise You, Holy Other 19
Holy Spirit
　O Loving Maker, Bless This Child, We Pray 37
　Waiting Now with Expectation 56
　We Come to Tell Our Stories 22
Holy Wisdom
　Awake to Work for Peace on Earth 7
　Celebrate Sophia's Birth 48
　Come, Celebrate and Sing 47
　Holy Wisdom Comes to Earth 44
　O Loving Maker, Bless This Child, We Pray 37
　Our Mother-Father, Friend and Source 15
　Sing of Peace, Holy Peace 49
　We Praise the Works of Wisdom 40
　When Will Justice Flow Like Waters? 8
　Wisdom Calls Us to Her Mission 23
Lady
　Ancient Wisdom, Mother of Earth 51
Life
　Come to Our World, O Christ-Sophia 45
Love
　Celebrate Our Life Together 20
Loving Friend
　O Holy Darkness, Source of Life 52
　We Gather Here to Pray 21
Loving Maker
　O Loving Maker, Bless This Child, We Pray 37
Loving Spirit
　Creation Calls to Us for Help 14
　Waiting Now with Expectation 56
Maker
　All the World with Beauty Shines 16
　Where Are You When We Need You? 29

Mary Magdalene
    Celebrate Sophia's Birth 48
Midwife
    Midwife Divine Is Bringing Life to Birth 26
Mother
    Ancient Wisdom, Mother of Earth 51
    O Loving Creator, We Labor with You 1,1a
Mother Christ
    Celebrate Our Life Together 20
Mother Eagle
    Mother Eagle in the Sky 28
Mother-Father
    All the World with Beauty Shines 16
    Our Mother-Father, Friend and Source 15
Mother Mary
    Celebrate Sophia's Birth 48
Musician Divine
    Composer of All the Music We Hear 42
Queen
    Ancient Wisdom, Mother of Earth 51
    Celebrate Sophia's Birth 48
Queen of Wisdom
    Holy Wisdom Comes to Earth 44
Renewing Spirit
    Creation Calls to Us for Help 14
Ruah
    Come, Ruah, Spirit, Bring New Life 12
    Ruah, Creator, Gave Birth to Us All 43
    Ruah, Spirit, Come Today 55
    Ruah, the Spirit, Gives Each One a Song 24
    Ruah, the Spirit-Source of All 4
Sacred Darkness
    Sacred Darkness Dwelling 18
Savior
    Wisdom Graciously Gives to All 27
Shekhinah
    Behold Shekhinah Leading 5
    Shekhinah Is Our Dwelling Place 9
Shepherd
    Our Shepherd Comes in Loving Care 35
    Our Shepherd Gives Us All We Need 32

Sister-Brother
    Sister-Brother, Peaceful Spirit 2
Sister-Brother-Friend
    Come, Easter People, Come, Rejoice 54
    Where Are You When We Need You? 29
Sister-Brother Spirit
    Celebrate Our Life Together 20
    Celebrate the Good Creation 41
    We Come to Tell Our Stories 22
    We Long to Dwell in Unity 17
Sophia
    Celebrate Sophia's Birth 48
    Come, Celebrate and Sing 47
    Come, Sophia, to Calm Our Souls 33
    Wisdom Graciously Gives to All 27
Source
    Our Mother-Father, Friend and Source 15
    Sacred Darkness Dwelling 18
Source of Life
    All the World with Beauty Shines 16
    O Holy Darkness, Source of Life 52
Spirit
    Celebrate the Good Creation 41
    Come, Ruah, Spirit, Bring New Life 12
    Creation Calls to Us for Help 14
    Great Creator, Bless This Child 38
    Ruah, Creator, Gave Birth to Us All 43
    Ruah, Spirit, Come Today 55
    Ruah, the Spirit, Gives Each One a Song 24
    Sister-Brother, Peaceful Spirit 2
    The Music Is Ringing 13
    We Long to Dwell in Unity 17
    Wisdom Calls Us to Her Mission 23
Spirit-Source
    Ruah, the Spirit-Source of All 4
Spirit of Oneness
    Ruah, the Spirit-Source of All 4
Star of Wisdom
    Star of Wonder, Star of Wisdom 50
Star of Wonder
    Star of Wonder, Star of Wisdom 50

Tree of Life
    Celebrate Sophia's Birth 48
    Celebrate the Works of Wisdom 10
    Holy Wisdom Comes to Earth 44

Truth
    Arise and Celebrate 6
    Come to Our World, O Christ-Sophia 45

Way
    Come, Celebrate and Sing 47
    Praise Wisdom in Our Hearts 3

Wisdom
    Awake to Work for Peace on Earth 7
    Celebrate the Works of Wisdom 10
    Come, Easter People, Come, Rejoice 54
    Come Now, and Follow Wisdom 25
    Come, Sophia, to Calm Our Souls 33
    Come to Our World, O Christ-Sophia 45
    How Long Will People Suffer? 30
    Sing of Peace, Holy Peace 49
    Praise Wisdom in Our Hearts 3
    We Praise the Works of Wisdom 40
    Wisdom Calls Us to Her Mission 23
    Wisdom Graciously Gives to All 27

Wisdom-Guide
    Wisdom Graciously Gives to All 27

Wisdom-Word
    We Are an Easter People 53

Wisdom, Sophia
    Wisdom, Sophia, Joins in Our Labor 11

DOUBT

Our Souls Find Rest and Comfort 34
Where Are You When We Need You? 29

EARTH DAY (see also Care of Creation)

All the World with Beauty Shines 16
Creation Calls to Us for Help 14
Our Mother-Father, Friend and Source 15

Sister-Brother, Peaceful Spirit 2
The Music Is Ringing 13

EASTER (see also Resurrection)

Come, Easter People, Come, Rejoice 54
We Are an Easter People 53

EPIPHANY

Ancient Wisdom, Mother of Earth 51
Behold Shekhinah Leading 5
O Holy Darkness, Source of Life 52
Star of Wonder, Star of Wisdom 50

ETERNAL LIFE

O Holy One, We Sing Your Praise 39
Our Shepherd Comes in Loving Care 35
Our Shepherd Gives Us All We Need 32
Sacred Darkness Dwelling 18
Wisdom Graciously Gives to All 27

FAITH AND TRUST

El Shaddai Will Come to Help Us 31
O Holy One, We Sing Your Praise 39
Our Shepherd Comes in Loving Care 35
Our Shepherd Gives Us All We Need 32
Our Souls Find Rest and Comfort 34
Shekhinah Is Our Dwelling Place 9
Wisdom Calls Us to Her Mission 23
Wisdom Graciously Gives to All 27

FORGIVENESS

Come Now, and Follow Wisdom 25
Holy Wisdom Comes to Earth 44
How Long Will People Suffer? 30
When Will Justice Flow Like Waters? 8

FREEDOM (see also Liberation)

Arise and Celebrate 6
Behold Shekhinah Leading 5
Celebrate the Good Creation 41
Celebrate the Works of Wisdom 10
Celebrate Sophia's Birth 48
Come to Free Us, Christ-Sophia 46
Come to Our World, O Christ-Sophia 45
Holy Wisdom Comes to Earth 44
Praise Wisdom in Our Hearts 3
Ruah, the Spirit-Source of All 4
Sister-Brother, Peaceful Spirit 2
Star of Wonder, Star of Wisdom 50
When Will Justice Flow Like Waters? 8

GIVING AND RECEIVING (see also Stewardship)

Celebrate Our Life Together 20
Celebrate the Works of Wisdom 10
Come, Easter People, Come, Rejoice 54
Composer of All the Music We Hear 42
O Loving Creator, We Labor with You 1,1a
Ruah, the Spirit, Gives Each One a Song 24
The Music Is Ringing 13
We Come to Tell Our Stories 22
Wisdom Calls Us to Her Mission 23
Wisdom Graciously Gives to All 27

GRACE

Come to Our World, O Christ-Sophia 45
O Holy Darkness, Source of Life 52
O Holy One, We Sing Your Praise 39
Ruah, the Spirit, Gives Each One a Song 24
Shekhinah Is Our Dwelling Place 9
Sister-Brother, Peaceful Spirit 2

GRIEF

Come, Christ-Sophia, Come 36

El Shaddai Will Come to Help Us 31
How Long Will People Suffer? 30
Our Shepherd Comes in Loving Care 35
Our Souls Find Rest and Comfort 34
Where Are You When We Need You? 29
Wisdom, Sophia, Joins in Our Labor 11

GUIDANCE AND CARE

Awake to Work for Peace on Earth 7
Behold Shekhinah Leading 5
El Shaddai Will Come to Help Us 31
Mother Eagle in the Sky 28
O Loving Maker, Bless This Child, We Pray 37
Our Mother-Father, Friend and Source 15
Our Shepherd Comes in Loving Care 35
Our Shepherd Gives Us All We Need 32
Star of Wonder, Star of Wisdom 50
Wisdom Calls Us to Her Mission 23

HEALING

Ancient Wisdom, Mother of Earth 51
Behold Shekhinah Leading 5
Celebrate Sophia's Birth 48
Celebrate the Good Creation 41
Come, Celebrate and Sing 47
Come, Christ-Sophia, Come 36
Come Now, and Follow Wisdom 25
Come, Sophia, to Calm Our Souls 33
Come to Our World, O Christ-Sophia 45
Composer of All the Music We Hear 42
El Shaddai Will Come to Help Us 31
Holy Wisdom Comes to Earth 44
Our Shepherd Comes in Loving Care 35
Our Shepherd Gives Us All We Need 32
Our Souls Find Rest and Comfort 34
Ruah, the Spirit, Gives Each One a Song 24
Sister-Brother, Peaceful Spirit 2
We Are an Easter People 53

We Gather Here to Pray 21
We Long to Dwell in Unity 17
When Will Justice Flow Like Waters? 8
Where Are You When We Need You? 29
Wisdom, Sophia, Joins in Our Labor 11

HOPE

Ancient Wisdom, Mother of Earth 51
Come, Celebrate and Sing 47
Come, Easter People, Come, Rejoice 54
Come Now, and Follow Wisdom 25
Come to Free Us, Christ-Sophia 46
Come to Our World, O Christ-Sophia 45
El Shaddai Will Come to Help Us 31
How Long Will People Suffer? 30
O Holy One, We Sing Your Praise 39
O Loving Creator, We Labor with You 1,1a
Our Shepherd Gives Us All We Need 32
Our Souls Find Rest and Comfort 34
Ruah, Spirit, Come Today 55
Ruah, the Spirit-Source of All 4
Shekhinah Is Our Dwelling Place 9
Sing of Peace, Holy Peace 49
Star of Wonder, Star of Wisdom 50
Waiting Now with Expectation 56
We Are an Easter People 53
We Gather Here to Pray 21
We Long to Dwell in Unity 17
Where Are You When We Need You? 29
Wisdom, Sophia, Joins in Our Labor 11

INCARNATION

Come, Celebrate and Sing 47
Come to Our World, O Christ-Sophia 45
Holy Wisdom Comes to Earth 44
Praise Wisdom in Our Hearts 3
Shekhinah Is Our Dwelling Place 9
We Praise You, Holy Other 19

INVITATION

Awake to Work for Peace on Earth 7
Come Now, and Follow Wisdom 25
Creation Calls to Us for Help 14
Wisdom Calls Us to Her Mission 23

JOY

O Holy One, We Sing Your Praise 39
Our Mother-Father, Friend and Source 15
Sing of Peace, Holy Peace 49
Waiting Now with Expectation 56
We Long to Dwell in Unity 17
We Praise the Works of Wisdom 40

LABOR

Come to Our World, O Christ-Sophia 45
Creation Calls to Us for Help 14
O Loving Creator, We Labor with You 1,1a
We Are an Easter People 53
Wisdom, Sophia, Joins in Our Labor 11

LAMENT

How Long Will People Suffer? 30
Where Are You When We Need You? 29

LENT

How Long Will People Suffer? 30
When Will Justice Flow Like Waters? 8

LIBERATION

Ancient Wisdom, Mother of Earth 51
Arise and Celebrate 6
Behold Shekhinah Leading 5
Come, Celebrate and Sing 47

Holy Wisdom Comes to Earth 44
How Long Will People Suffer? 30
Ruah, Spirit, Come Today 55
Shekhinah Is Our Dwelling Place 9
Waiting Now with Expectation 56
We Come to Tell Our Stories 22
We Praise You, Holy Other 19
Wisdom, Sophia, Joins in Our Labor 11

LOVE

Ancient Wisdom, Mother of Earth 51
Behold Shekhinah Leading 5
Celebrate the Good Creation 41
Come, Sophia, to Calm Our Souls 33
Come to Free Us, Christ-Sophia 46
El Shaddai Will Come to Help Us 31
Great Creator, Bless This Child 38
Mother Eagle in the Sky 28
O Holy One, We Sing Your Praise 39
O Loving Maker, Bless This Child, We Pray 37
Praise Wisdom in Our Hearts 3
Ruah, Creator, Gave Birth to Us All 43
Ruah, Spirit, Come Today 55
Shekhinah Is Our Dwelling Place 9
Sing of Peace, Holy Peace 49
Sister-Brother, Peaceful Spirit 2
We Come to Tell Our Stories 22
We Praise You, Holy Other 19
Wisdom Calls Us to Her Mission 23
Wisdom Graciously Gives to All 27

MINISTRY

Celebrate Our Life Together 20
Come to Free Us, Christ-Sophia 46
Composer of All the Music We Hear 42
Great Creator, Bless This Child 38
O Loving Creator, We Labor with You 1,1a
O Loving Maker, Bless This Child, We Pray 37
When Will Justice Flow Like Waters? 8

MIRACLE

Great Creator, Bless This Child 38
Sacred Darkness Dwelling 18
Star of Wonder, Star of Wisdom 50
The Music Is Ringing 13
We Are an Easter People 53

MISSION

Come, Christ-Sophia, Come 36
Come, Easter People, Come, Rejoice 54
Come Now, and Follow Wisdom 25
Come to Free Us, Christ-Sophia 46
Mother Eagle in the Sky 28
Sister-Brother, Peaceful Spirit 2
Star of Wonder, Star of Wisdom 50
Waiting Now with Expectation 56
We Are an Easter People 53
Wisdom Calls Us to Her Mission 23
Wisdom Graciously Gives to All 27

NEW CREATION

Celebrate Our Life Together 20
Celebrate the Works of Wisdom 10
Come Now, and Follow Wisdom 25
Come to Free Us, Christ-Sophia 46
Come to Our World, O Christ-Sophia 45
How Long Will People Suffer? 30
O Loving Creator, We Labor with You 1,1a
Ruah, the Spirit, Gives Each One a Song 24
Sing of Peace, Holy Peace 49
Star of Wonder, Star of Wisdom 50
The Music Is Ringing 13
We Are an Easter People 53
We Praise You, Holy Other 19

NEW LIFE

Celebrate Our Life Together 20

Come, Celebrate and Sing	47
Come, Ruah, Spirit, Bring New Life	12
O Loving Maker, Bless This Child, We Pray	37
We Are An Easter People	53
Wisdom Graciously Gives to All	27

ONENESS

Sacred Darkness Dwelling	18
Sister-Brother, Peaceful Spirit	2
The Music Is Ringing	13
We Gather Here to Pray	21
We Long to Dwell in Unity	17
We Praise You, Holy Other	19

PARTNERSHIP

All the World with Beauty Shines	16
Arise and Celebrate	6
Celebrate Our Life Together	20
Come to Free Us, Christ-Sophia	46
Come to Our World, O Christ-Sophia	45
O Loving Creator, We Labor with You	1,1a
Sister-Brother, Peaceful Spirit	2
We Gather Here to Pray	21

PEACE

Ancient Wisdom, Mother of Earth	51
Arise and Celebrate	6
Awake to Work for Peace on Earth	7
Behold Shekhinah Leading	5
Celebrate Our Life Together	20
Celebrate Sophia's Birth	48
Celebrate the Good Creation	41
Celebrate the Works of Wisdom	10
Come, Celebrate and Sing	47
Come, Christ-Sophia, Come	36
Come, Easter People, Come, Rejoice	54
Come Now, and Follow Wisdom	25
Come, Ruah, Spirit, Bring New Life	12

Come, Sophia, to Calm Our Souls 33
Come to Free Us, Christ-Sophia 46
Come to Our World, O Christ-Sophia 45
El Shaddai Will Come to Help Us 31
Holy Wisdom Comes to Earth 44
How Long Will People Suffer? 30
O Holy Darkness, Source of Life 52
O Loving Creator, We Labor with You 1,1a
Our Shepherd Comes in Loving Care 35
Our Shepherd Gives Us All We Need 32
Our Souls Find Rest and Comfort 34
Praise Wisdom in Our Hearts 3
Ruah, Spirit, Come Today 55
Ruah, the Spirit, Gives Each One a Song 24
Ruah, the Spirit-Source of All 4
Shekhinah Is Our Dwelling Place 9
Sing of Peace, Holy Peace 49
Sister-Brother, Peaceful Spirit 2
Star of Wonder, Star of Wisdom 50
We Are an Easter People 53
We Gather Here to Pray 21
We Long to Dwell in Unity 17
When Will Justice Flow Like Waters? 8
Wisdom Calls Us to Her Mission 23
Wisdom Graciously Gives to All 27
Wisdom, Sophia, Joins in Our Labor 11

PENTECOST

Ruah, Spirit, Come Today 55
Waiting Now with Expectation 56

POWER

Awake to Work for Peace on Earth 7
Behold Shekhinah Leading 5
Come, Easter People, Come, Rejoice 54
Come Now, and Follow Wisdom 25
Come to Our World, O Christ-Sophia 45
Composer of All the Music We Hear 42
Holy Wisdom Comes to Earth 44

O Holy One, We Sing Your Praise 39
Our Mother-Father, Friend and Source 15
Ruah, Spirit, Come Today 55
Ruah, the Spirit-Source of All 4
Shekhinah Is Our Dwelling Place 9
Sister-Brother, Peaceful Spirit 2
Waiting Now with Expectation 56
We Are an Easter People 53
Wisdom, Sophia, Joins in Our Labor 11

PRAISE (see also Thanksgiving)

Composer of All the Music We Hear 42
Holy Wisdom Comes to Earth 44
O Holy One, We Sing Your Praise 39
Praise Wisdom in Our Hearts 3
Ruah, Creator, Gave Birth to Us All 43
We Long to Dwell in Unity 17
We Praise the Works of Wisdom 40
We Praise You, Holy Other 19

PRAYER

Come, Sophia, to Calm Our Souls 33
Composer of All the Music We Hear 42
Great Creator, Bless This Child 38
Mother Eagle in the Sky 28
O Holy One, We Sing Your Praise 39
O Loving Maker, Bless This Child, We Pray 37
Our Mother-Father, Friend and Source 15
Sister-Brother, Peaceful Spirit 2
Star of Wonder, Star of Wisdom 50
We Praise You, Holy Other 19
When Will Justice Flow Like Waters? 8
Where Are You When We Need You? 29

RENEWAL

Come, Sophia, to Calm Our Souls 33
Creation Calls to Us for Help 14
Our Shepherd Comes in Loving Care 35

Our Shepherd Gives Us All We Need	32
Praise Wisdom in Our Hearts	3
We Praise the Works of Wisdom	40

REPENTANCE (see Forgiveness)

RESURRECTION (see also Easter)

Come, Easter People, Come, Rejoice	54
We Are an Easter People	53

SOCIAL JUSTICE

Ancient Wisdom, Mother of Earth	51
Arise and Celebrate	6
Awake to Work for Peace on Earth	7
Behold Shekhinah Leading	5
Celebrate Our Life Together	20
Celebrate the Good Creation	41
Celebrate the Works of Wisdom	10
Come, Celebrate and Sing	47
Come to Free Us, Christ-Sophia	46
Come to Our World, O Christ-Sophia	45
Holy Wisdom Comes to Earth	44
How Long Will People Suffer?	30
O Loving Creator, We Labor with You	1,1a
Ruah, Spirit, Come Today	55
Ruah, the Spirit-Source of All	4
Sacred Darkness Dwelling	18
Sing of Peace, Holy Peace	49
We Come to Tell Our Stories	22
We Praise You, Holy Other	19
When Will Justice Flow Like Waters?	8
Wisdom Calls Us to Her Mission	23
Wisdom Graciously Gives to All	27

STEWARDSHIP (see also Giving and Receiving; Creation)

Creation Calls to Us for Help	14
Our Mother-Father, Friend and Source	15
Ruah, the Spirit, Gives Each One a Song	24

Ruah, the Spirit-Source of All 4
We Long to Dwell in Unity 17

THANKSGIVING

Composer of all the Music We Hear 42
O Holy One, We Sing Your Praise 39
Our Mother-Father, Friend and Source 15
Ruah, Creator, Gave Birth to Us All 43
We Praise the Works of Wisdom 40

TRINITY

Composer of All the Music We Hear 42
O Loving Maker, Bless This Child, We Pray 37
Our Mother-Father, Friend and Source 15

TRUTH

Behold Shekhinah Leading 5
Come, Celebrate and Sing 47
Come, Christ-Sophia, Come 36
Come to Our World, O Christ-Sophia 45
Holy Wisdom Comes to Earth 44
How Long Will People Suffer? 30
Shekhinah Is Our Dwelling Place 9
Star of Wonder, Star of Wisdom 50
When Will Justice Flow Like Waters? 8
Wisdom Calls Us to Her Mission 23

UNITY AND DIVERSITY

All the World with Beauty Shines 16
Celebrate Our Life Together 20
Celebrate the Good Creation 41
O Loving Creator, We Labor with You 1,1a
Ruah, the Spirit, Gives Each One a Song 24
We Come to Tell Our Stories 22
We Gather Here to Pray 21
We Long to Dwell in Unity 17
We Praise You, Holy Other 19

VISION

Behold Shekhinah Leading 5
Celebrate the Works of Wisdom 10
Come Now, and Follow Wisdom 25
Come, Sophia, to Calm Our Souls 33
Come to Our World, O Christ-Sophia 45
O Loving Creator, We Labor with You 1,1a
Ruah, the Spirit, Gives Each One a Song 24
Ruah, the Spirit-Source of All 4
Shekhinah Is Our Dwelling Place 9
Star of Wonder, Star of Wisdom 50
The Music Is Ringing 13
Waiting Now with Expectation 56
We Are an Easter People 53
We Come to Tell Our Stories 22
We Praise You, Holy Other 19

WHOLENESS

Awake to Work for Peace on Earth 7
Behold Shekhinah Leading 5
Composer of All the Music We Hear 42
O Holy Darkness, Source of Life 52
O Loving Maker, Bless This Child, We Pray 37
Our Shepherd Comes in Loving Care 35
We Gather Here to Pray 21

INDEX OF SCRIPTURE REFERENCES

Genesis

1 . . . . 43, 52
1:1-2 . . . . 12, 55
1:1-27 4
1:26-27 . . . . 16, 37, 38, 41
1:31 41
49:25 . . . . 31, 34

Exodus

29:45 . . . . 5, 9
40:34-38 . . . . 5, 9

Deuteronomy

32:11-12 28

Psalms

19:1-4 . . . . 13, 15
22:1-2 29
22:9-10 26
23 . . . . 32, 35
33:1-3 42
44:23-25 29
65:6-13 16
71:14-24 39
77:1-5 29
84 35
85:10 4
96:1 24
104:1-30 40
104:5-32 14
104:16-25 15
104:30 4
108:4 33
133:1 . . . . 2, 17
136:1-9 16
139:11-12 52
144:9 24
148:1-12 16

Proverbs

1 10
1:20-23 . . . . 3, 27, 44, 47
1:20-24 . . . . 7, 30
1:20-25 25
3 10
3:13-15 40
3:13-17 49
3:13-18 . . . . 3, 7, 8, 11, 25,
27, 30, 44, 48, 51

3:17 . . . . 37, 46, 54
3:17-18. . . . . 33, 45, 47, 50
8 10
8:1-20. 44
8:20. . . . . 7, 23
8:23-31 51
9:1, 5-6 40

Isaiah

30:29. 24
40:25. 19
42:14. . . . . 1, 1a, 11
45:3. . . . . 18, 52
49:15. 31
55:9. 19
55:12. 17
66:13. . . . . 1, 1a, 31, 34

Amos

5:24. 8

Micah

6:8. 20

Matthew

11:28-30. 36
23:37 . . . . 20, 30, 44
25:40. . . . . 53, 54
28:20. 53

Luke

4:18-19. . . . . 6, 8, 20, 41

John

1:1. 53
8:32. 6

14:6. 45
15:13. 53

Acts

2:1-18. 55, 56

1 Corinthians

1:24 . . . . 45, 46, 53
12:4-11. 20
12:12-31. 21
14:15. 42

2 Corinthians

5:17 . . . . 1,1a, 13, 45, 46, 49

Galatians

3:28. . . . . 6, 21
5:22-23. . . . . 2, 12, 56
6:2. 8

Ephesians

4:32. 38

2 Timothy

1:7. 37

James

3:17. 25
3:13-18. 23

Revelation

21:5. 22

INDEX OF COMPOSERS, AUTHORS, AND SOURCES

Adam, Adolphe (1803-1856), 45
Angell, Warren M. (1907-2006), 48
Atkinson, Frederick C. (1841-1897), 24
Bach, Johann Sebastian (1685-1750), 29, 39
Bain, James L. (c. 1840-1925), 35
Barnby, Joseph (1838-1896), 21
Beethoven, Ludwig van (1770-1827), 10, 20
Bliss, Philip P. (1838-1876), 27
Dare, Elkanah Kelsay (1782-1826), 14
Doane, William H. (1832-1915), 36
Emerson, Luther Orlando (1820-1915), 41
English folk melody, 7
Finnish melody, 19
Fischer, William G. (1835-1912), 22
French carol, 48
Gauntlett, Henry J. (1805-1876), 31
German melody, 47
Gesangbuch, Wittenberg (1784), 5
Gruber, Franz (1787-1863), 49
Hassler, Hans Leo (1564-1612), 29
Hatton, John (c. 1710-1793), 54
Hebrew melody, 12
Holst, Gustav (1874-1934), 18, 50
Hopkins, Edward J. (1818-1901), 37
Hopkins, Jr., John Henry (1820-1891), 51

Irvine, Jessie S. (1836-1887), 32
Kocher, Conrad (1786-1872), 38
Luther, Martin (1483-1546), 39
MacMillan, Ernest (1893-1973), 44
Maker, Frederick C. (1844-1927), 30
Mendelssohn, Felix (1809-1847), 33
Monk, William Henry (1823-1889), 38
Parry, Joseph (1841-1903), 55
Peace, Albert L. (1844-1912), 52
Piae Cantiones (1582), 44
Polish carol, 46
Prichard, Rowland H. (1811-1887), 56
Schultz, Larry E. (1965-), 1, 3, 17, 19, 23, 26, 27, 28, 35, 42, 43, 46
Schulz, Johann A. P. (1747-1800), 40
Schumann, Robert (1810-1856), 9
Shaw, Martin F. (1875-1958), 16
Sibelius, Jean (1865-1957), 26
Smart, Henry T. (1813-1879), 53
Tochter Sion, Cologne (1741), 2
Traditional English melody, 15, 16, 17
Traditional Gaelic melody, 11
Traditional Spanish melody, 3
Traditional Welsh melody, 41
Vaughan Williams, Ralph (1872-1958), 7, 15

Venua, Frederick M.A. (1788-1872), 4
Walter, William H. (1825-1893), 6
Welsh hymn tune, 1a
Welsh melody, 13
Wesley, Samuel S. (1810-1876), 25
White, B.F. (1800-1879), 23
Williams, Thomas John (1869-1944), 8
Wyeth's *Repository of Sacred Music, Part Second*, 14

ALPHABETICAL INDEX OF TUNES

ABERYSTWYTH, 7.7.7.7 D 55
ADAIR, 7.7.7.7 28
AR HYD Y NOS, 8.4.8.4.8.8.8.4 41
ASH GROVE, 12.11.12.11 D 13
AURELIA, 7.6.7.6 D 25
BEACH SPRING, 8.7.8.7 D 23
BIRMINGHAM, Irregular..33
BROTHER JAMES' AIR, 8.6.8.6.8.6 35
BUNESSAN, 5.5.5.4 D..11
CANONBURY, 8.8.8.8 (LM) 9
CANTIQUE DE NOEL, Irregular 45
CRANHAM, 6.5.6.5 D..18
CRIMOND, 8.6.8.6 (CM) 32
DIX, 7.7.7.7 with refrain 38
DUKE STREET, 8.8.8.8 (LM) 54
EBENEZER, 8.7.8.7 D 8
EIN' FESTE BURG, 8.7.8.7.6.6.6.6.7 39
ELLACOMBE, 7.6.7.6 D 5
ELLERS, 10.10.10.10 37
FESTAL SONG, 6.6.8.6 6
FINLANDIA, 10.10.10.10.10.10 26

FOREST GREEN, 8.6.8.6 D (CMD) 15
GLORIA, 7.7.7.7 with refrain..48
HANKEY, 7.6.7.6 D with refrain..22
HYFRYDOL, 8.7.8.7 D 56
HYMN TO JOY, 8.7.8.7 D..10, 20
IN DULCI JUBILO, 6.6.7.7.7.8.5.5 47
IRBY, 8.7.8.7.7.7..31
KINGS OF ORIENT, 8.8.8.6 with refrain 51
KINGSFOLD, 8.6.8.6 D (CMD) 7
LANCASHIRE, 7.6.7.6 D 53
LAUDES DOMINI, 6.6.6.6.6.6 21
MADRID, 6.6.6.6 D 3
MORE LOVE TO THEE, 6.4.6.4.6.6.4.4 36
MORECAMBE, 10.10.10.10 24
MORNING SONG, 8.6.8.6.8.6 14
NYLAND, 7.6.7.6 D..19
O WALY WALY, 8.8.8.8 (LM)...17
PARK STREET, 8.8.8.8.8 4
PASSION CHORALE, 7.6.7.6 D 29
ROYAL OAK, 7.6.7.6 with refrain...16
RUAH, 10.10.10.10 43
SHALOM, Irregular 12
ST. CHRISTOPHER, Irregular 30
ST. DENIO, 11.11.11.11 ....1a
ST. MARGARET, 8.8.8.8.6 52
STILLE NACHT, Irregular..49
TEMPUS ADEST FLORIDUM, 7.6.7.6 D 44
THAXTED, 14.14.15.14.14.14 50
TIMBERLAKE, 10.10.11.11...42
VESTA, 11.11.11.11... 1
W ZLOBIE LEZY, 8.7.8.7.8.8.7 46
WEISSE FLAGGEN, 8.7.8.7 D 2
WHITFIELD, 7.6.7.6 D..34
WIR PFLUGEN, 7.6.7.6 D with refrain 40
WORDS OF LIFE, Irregular 27

METRICAL INDEX OF TUNES

5.5.5.4 D
BUNESSAN, 11

6.4.6.4.6.6.4.4
MORE LOVE TO THEE, 36

6.5.6.5 D
CRANHAM, 18

6.6.6.6 D
MADRID, 3

6.6.6.6.6.6
LAUDES DOMINI, 21

6.6.7.7.7.8.5.5
IN DULCI JUBILO, 47

6.6.8.6
FESTAL SONG, 6

7.6.7.6 with refrain
ROYAL OAK, 16

7.6.7.6 D
AURELIA, 25
ELLACOMBE, 5
LANCASHIRE, 53
NYLAND, 19
PASSION CHORALE, 29
TEMPUS ADEST FLORIDUM, 44
WHITFIELD, 34

7.6.7.6 D with refrain
HANKEY, 22
WIR PFLUGEN, 40

7.7.7.7
ADAIR, 28

7.7.7.7 with refrain
DIX, 38
GLORIA, 48

7.7.7.7 D
ABERYSTWYTH, 55

8.4.8.4.8.8.8.4
AR HYD Y NOS, 41

8.6.8.6 (CM)
CRIMOND, 32

8.6.8.6 D (CMD)
FOREST GREEN, 15
KINGSFOLD, 7

8.6.8.6.8.6
BROTHER JAMES' AIR, 35
MORNING SONG, 14

8.7.8.7 D
BEACH SPRING, 23
EBENEZER, 8
HYFRYDOL, 56
HYMN TO JOY, 10, 20
WEISSE FLAGGEN, 2

8.7.8.7.6.6.6.6.7
EIN' FESTE BURG, 39

8.7.8.7.7.7
IRBY, 31

8.7.8.7.8.8.7
W ZLOBIE LEZY, 46

8.8.8.6 with refrain
KINGS OF ORIENT, 51

8.8.8.8 (LM)
CANONBURY, 9
DUKE STREET, 54
O WALY WALY, 17

8.8.8.8.6
ST. MARGARET, 52

8.8.8.8.8
PARK STREET, 4

10.10.10.10
ELLERS, 37
MORECAMBE, 24
RUAH, 43

10.10.10.10.10.10
FINLANDIA, 26

10.10.11.11
TIMBERLAKE, 42

11.11.11.11
ST. DENIO, 1a
VESTA, 1

12.11.12.11 D
ASH GROVE, 13

14.14.15.14.14.14
THAXTED, 50

Irregular
BIRMINGHAM, 33
CANTIQUE DE NOEL, 45
SHALOM, 12
ST. CHRISTOPHER, 30
STILLE NACHT, 49
WORDS OF LIFE, 27

INDEX OF TITLES

All the World with Beauty Shines	16
Ancient Wisdom, Mother of Earth	51
Arise and Celebrate	6
Awake to Work for Peace on Earth	7
Behold Shekhinah Leading	5
Celebrate Our Life Together	20
Celebrate Sophia's Birth	48
Celebrate the Good Creation	41
Celebrate the Works of Wisdom	10
Come, Celebrate and Sing	47
Come, Christ-Sophia, Come	36
Come, Easter People, Come, Rejoice	54
Come Now, and Follow Wisdom	25
Come, Ruah, Spirit, Bring New Life	12
Come, Sophia, to Calm our Souls	33
Come to Free Us, Christ-Sophia	46
Come to Our World, O Christ-Sophia	45
Composer of All the Music We Hear	42
Creation Calls to Us for Help	14
El Shaddai Will Come to Help Us	31
Great Creator, Bless This Child	38
Holy Wisdom Comes to Earth	44
How Long Will People Suffer?	30
Midwife Divine Is Bringing Life to Birth	26
Mother Eagle in the Sky	28
O Holy Darkness, Source of Life	52

O Holy One, We Sing Your Praise	39
O Loving Creator, We Labor with You	1, 1a
O Loving Maker, Bless This Child, We Pray	37
Our Mother-Father, Friend and Source	15
Our Shepherd Comes in Loving Care	35
Our Shepherd Gives Us All We Need	32
Our Souls Find Rest and Comfort	34
Praise Wisdom in Our Hearts	3
Ruah, Creator, Gave Birth to Us All	43
Ruah, Spirit, Come Today	55
Ruah, the Spirit, Gives Each One a Song	24
Ruah, the Spirit-Source of All	4
Sacred Darkness Dwelling	18
Shekhinah Is Our Dwelling Place	9
Sing of Peace, Holy Peace	49
Sister-Brother, Peaceful Spirit	2
Star of Wonder, Star of Wisdom	50
The Music Is Ringing	13
Waiting Now with Expectation	56
We Are an Easter People	53
We Come to Tell Our Stories	22
We Gather Here to Pray	21
We Long to Dwell in Unity	17
We Praise the Works of Wisdom	40
We Praise You, Holy Other	19
When Will Justice Flow Like Waters?	8
Where Are You When We Need You?	29
Wisdom Calls Us to Her Mission	23
Wisdom Graciously Gives to All	27
Wisdom, Sophia, Joins in Our Labor	11

Books From Jann Aldredge-Clanton & Eakin Press

Breaking Free: The Story of a Feminist Baptist Minister
Jann Aldredge-Clanton didn't start out as a reformer. When she was a pre-teen, she almost starved herself to death trying to fit into the culture's feminine mold. In high school she felt inadequate because she never won a beauty crown, even though she graduated at the top of her class. Slowly, she began waking up to her own voice, and became one of the first women ever to be ordained as a Baptist minister in the South.

In Search of the Christ-Sophia: An Inclusive Christology for Liberating Christians
presents powerful biblical and theological support for a Divine Feminine image buried in Christianity. The popularity of The Da Vinci Code demonstrates the widespread hunger for the lost Sacred Feminine. This book resurrects Sophia (Wisdom) and connects Her to Jesus Christ.

Hymnals & Songbooks

Inclusive Hymns for Liberating Christians
These hymns will lift the heart, invigorate the mind, and enliven the spirit. The wide variety of biblical divine names and images in this hymnbook will contribute to belief in the sacredness of all people and all creation. Peace and justice flow from this belief.

Inclusive Hymns for Liberation, Peace, and Justice
Words we sing in worship have great power to shape our beliefs and actions. This is the second collection of hymns by Jann Aldredge-Clanton with composer Larry E. Schultz. These hymns, like those in the first collection, will contribute to an expansive theology and an ethic of equality and justice in human relationships.

Earth Transformed with Music! Inclusive Songs for Worship
Music has great power to touch the heart and change the world. Words we sing in worship shape our beliefs and actions. The inclusive songs in this collection will contribute to social justice, peace, equality, and expansive spiritual experience. This collection includes all new songs, most to widely-known tunes and some to new tunes.

Inclusive Songs for Resistance & Social Action
Music empowers action for social change. Music stirs our spirits and embeds words in our memories. Words shape our values that drive our actions. Singing our beliefs in justice, peace, and equality will move us to transform our world. *Inclusive Songs for Resistance & Social Action* will contribute to gender, racial, economic, environmental, and other justice movements.

Inclusive Songs from the Heart of Gospel
Music has great power to spread the good news of peace, justice, liberation, and abundant life for all people. This new song collection proclaims this good news with lyrics inclusive in gender and race and with themes of social justice and peacemaking. The title of this collection, *Inclusive Songs from the Heart* of Gospel, comes from our choice of gospel music tunes for most of our texts.

Eakin Press
PO Box 331779 • Fort Worth, Texas 76163 • 817-344-7036
www.EakinPress.com
A Subsidiary of Wild Horse Media Group

www.ingramcontent.com/pod-product-compliance
Lightning Source LLC
Chambersburg PA
CBHW080639170426
43200CB00015B/2898